Sam Cowley
LEGENDARY LAWMAN

Sam Cowley
LEGENDARY LAWMAN

By Richard L. Emery

Forward by Sam Cowley, Jr.

Springville, Utah

Copyright © 2004 Richard L. Emery

All Rights Reserved.

No part of this book may be reproduced in any form whatsoever, whether by graphic, visual, electronic, film, microfilm, tape recording, or any other means, without prior written permission of the author, except in the case of brief passages embodied in critical reviews and articles.

ISBN: 1-55517-741-7
e. 1

Published by Cedar Fort Inc.
www.cedarfort.com

Distributed by:

Cover design by Nicole Cunningham
Cover design © 2004 by Lyle Mortimer

Printed in the United States of America
10 9 8 7 6 5 4 3 2 1

Printed on acid-free paper

Library of Congress Control Number: 2004104252

"I have said many times that Sam Cowley was the bravest man I ever knew."

— J. Edgar Hoover

Dedicated to the late Dr. John Forbes, history professor at Blackburn College, my mentor and friend who got me hooked on history early on.

CONTENTS

Foreword xii
Preface xvii
1—Sam's Early Years 1
2—Sam Joins the FBI 7
3—The Demise of "Pretty Boy" Floyd 13
4—The Net is Closing 19
5—The Barker-Karpis Kidnappings 23
6—The Hunt for Dillinger 31
7—The Rhinelander Rendezvous 37
8—The Woman in Red 43
9—The Gangster with the Baby Face 49
10—Too Tough for Big Al 53
11—Cowley vs. Nelson 59
12—The Aftermath 65
13—The Trial 73
Epilogue 77
Appendix 83
Bibliography 95
Acknowledgments 97
About the Author 98

FOREWORD

Because I was just eight months old when my father was killed in the shootout with "Baby Face" Nelson, I had no firsthand knowledge of him. I did listen intently to the stories told by my mother and relatives and was able to read a great deal about my father in books, magazines and some newspaper accounts. But this information came in bits and scraps and mainly focused on the two most famous cases—John Dillinger and "Baby Face" Nelson.

I really didn't fully appreciate the overall history of my father's broad career in the FBI and his involvement, by special assignment, in many other prominent gangster cases. Also new to me was the extent of preparation and work required for the Dillinger and "Baby Face" Nelson captures. I found the discussion of the development and growth of the FBI in scope and criminal jurisdiction during this early period very interesting.

When I was contacted by Richard Emery as he was working on this book designed to tell the story of Dad's entire life, I was eager to help in any way I could. I was especially pleased with the broad range of far-flung sources this book accesses—including a wealth of information in the archives of Utah State University, my father's alma mater.

By gathering together the many facets of Dad's story, this book will be a useful resource to my father's posterity for generations, helping them understand their ancestor and his role in helping to make their country safer in a greatly troubling time. It takes a lot of work to study and cull all the records, raw data, and archival sources that Richard ferreted out, bringing together the important facts of Father's youth, schooling, mission, and far-ranging FBI career.

Over the years I have read many often conflicting accounts of my father's involvement in the Dillinger case.

The problem of conflicting versions of the story increased the difficulty of Richard's work. It was an enormous task to examine the many resources he pursued, sifting through the various and conflicting versions, digesting the enormous collection of materials, and determining which of the conflicting versions was the most reliable and consistent with the primary sources. This book does a good job in clearing up the record.

I extend heartfelt thanks to Richard for this book on behalf of his expanding posterity, who in its reading will get to know him and feel a certain pride in their heritage.

—Samuel P. Cowley, Jr.

PREFACE

Writing this book has been a labor of love. Through extensive research, I have put together what I believe to be a straightforward and true account of Sam Cowley's life and times.

Literature and film often focus on the gangsters and their thrilling, reckless, and devastating actions during those lawless years. Yet little has been written of the brave lawmen who rounded them up and took them out of circulation, allowing the American public to regain some measure of freedom and security. This book is my attempt to give credit to these fearless guardians for ridding our nation of lawless, roaming murderers, thus restoring our right to freedom from fear.

Sam Cowley set his mind on a career in law enforcement. He firmly believed in the Church's Twelfth Article of Faith: *We believe in being subject to kings, rulers, presidents, and magistrates, in obeying, honoring and sustaining the law.*. Sam was known to put in 16-hour days with the FBI★, spend a good deal of time with his family, and still teach Sunday School. FBI Director J. Edgar Hoover soon noticed Sam's potential and gave him many opportunities to prove himself. His rapid advancement in the Bureau was due partly to his love of his job, only outdone by his great love for his wife and two small boys. This quiet-mannered young lawyer became Hoover's troubleshooter for crime's hot spots wherever they developed; his job was more hazardous than most in the Bureau.

Due to Cowley's natural reticence and his agreement with the culture of ascribing success to the Justice Department in general rather than to individual agents competing for recognition, the public heard little of him. Yet it was he who laid the groundwork for the pursuit of John Dillinger, Charles "Pretty Boy" Floyd, Ma Barker and "Baby Face" Nelson—the nation's most feared public enemies. Melvin Purvis was the agent in charge of the Chicago field office, but it was Cowley who commanded these operations.

Even though he shunned the limelight, Sam Cowley deserves recognition for the profound accomplishments he achieved during his short career in the service of his country.

So here is Sam Cowley, born of goodly parents, son of one apostle of the Lord, and brother to another. Sam was nurtured in the gospel of Jesus Christ from the cradle. Missionary, lawyer, G-man extraordinaire. He was a gallant elder in the Church of Jesus Christ of Latter-day Saints, and when he had a job to do, he did it well. He was a man of courage and commitment, a guardian of truth and human rights and a dreadful nemesis to all the underworld.

This is the story of a valiant soldier in the Royal Army of God who remained true to his high standards through his final hours (SPC, 21-24).

—Richard L. Emery

*The proper name for this agency was the United States Department of Justice, Division of Investigation, until 1935 when the name was changed to the Federal Bureau of Investigation. For convenience and ease of understanding, the agency shall be referred to throughout the book as the FBI or the Bureau.

Samuel Parkinson Cowley
1899-1934

1

Sam's Early Years

During the lawless years of the Great Depression, gangsters roamed the Midwest, robbing banks, killing innocent citizens and police officers. Some of the toughest of these criminals were John Dillinger and Lester Gillis, otherwise known as George 'Baby Face' Nelson. Dillinger topped the government's Public Enemy list, with Nelson following close behind.

One of the bravest and most dedicated law officers of that era was FBI Inspector Sam Cowley. The public was growing alarmed at the many unsuccessful attempts to capture the bank bandits and cop killers. Sam was assigned by FBI Director J. Edgar Hoover to bring the lot of them to justice. Sam was instrumental in bringing down 'Pretty Boy' Floyd, Ma Barker and her sons, the notorious John Dillinger, and one super crook— 'Baby Face' Nelson.

According to Hoover, Sam "was in full charge of all investigative activity directed toward the location and apprehension of gangster John Dillinger, . . . the supervision of the Bremer kidnapping case, the Kansas City Massacre investigations . . . and the apprehension of Lester Gillis aka George 'Baby Face' Nelson (Hoover, Marriott Letter).

Born July 28, 1899 in Franklin, Idaho, to Latter-day Saint parents Matthias Foss Cowley and Luella Parkinson, Samuel Parkinson Cowley was the fifth son in a family of nine sons and six daughters. Sam's character was molded from birth by loving and caring parents and by his twelve siblings.

Sam was born of a plural marriage, a practice somewhat widespread among Latter-day Saints in the 1800s.

Matthias F. Cowley, Sam's father, served as a missionary for the Church, converted and baptized many souls, and traveled extensively later as a member of the Quorum of Twelve Apostles. He became a prolific writer of Church literature.

Matthew Cowley, a noted apostle of the Church who had served many years in New Zealand, was Sam's half-brother, born of the union of Matthias F. Cowley and Abie Hyde in Preston, Idaho, August 2, 1897.

Sam's family moved to Preston, Idaho when he was six years old. He attended the Oneida Stake Academy there. The need for academies such as this grew out of the anti-Latter-day Saint laws that came to a head with the Edmunds-Tucker Act in 1887, banning the teaching of LDS doctrine in public schools and prohibiting Church members from serving on school boards.

Church President Wilford Woodruff directed that a board of education should be organized in each of the stakes of the Church, providing religious training for LDS youth. Notable alumni from the Oneida academy include Harold B. Lee and Ezra Taft Benson, future presidents of the Church.

The Church abandoned the academy system in 1922 when students returned to public education. Sam was baptized into The Church of Jesus Christ of Latter-day Saints on his eighth birthday, 23 July, 1907. At age 11, Sam moved to Logan, Utah, pursuing his studies at grade schools and Logan High. At 12 he was duly ordained a deacon 23 October, 1911, and a teacher at age 15. He faithfully fulfilled his priesthood duties, becoming a counselor in the presidencies of both quorums.

Sam used his summer vacations to earn money by mowing lawns in Logan and working for the Utah Agricultural College.

At age 17 Sam was ordained an elder in the Melchizedek Priesthood and left to serve a Church mission to the Hawaiian Islands. The mission would last three years and nine months.

"Sam soon mastered the Hawaiian language," according to his brother-in-law, Edgar B. Brossard. "He was versatile in gospel doctrine and Church history. He always spoke with affection for the Hawaiian people. Their humility and sincerity appealed to him. He liked the simple refrains of their music." He baptized converts, blessed children, and administered to the sick and afflicted. He labored in the building of a chapel in Laie, and tirelessly helped raise funds for the construction of the Hawaiian Temple. He gave of his own money and time in the project.

Sam Cowley
served a mission to the
Hawaiian Islands.

Before his release from the Hawaiian Mission, he visited each island in the group, including Leper Island, the home of many afflicted with this horrible disease. He was deeply impressed with the patience and cheerfulness of the leprosy victims as they sang and played their ukuleles. It was a lesson in patience and fortitude for Sam. He saw them as an example to be followed by all people.

Sam's Church mission to Hawaii taught him numerous lessons about people; how to deal with them, how to love them, and how to teach them to love themselves. Most Church missions for young elders last for two years, but for Sam it was nearly four. His sacrifice of time and funds taught him many lessons that proved invaluable later in life.

When Sam returned to Logan in the fall of 1921, he enrolled in the Agricultural College, majoring in economics. He helped earn his way through school by working for the institution. There is a picture of Sam Cowley in the 1923 edition of the *Buzzer*, the Utah Agriculture College Yearbook. Sam is standing in a suit, tie, and cap with his arms half-folded as if he can't quite wait for the camera before he gets on to his next task. The following text sits next to the picture: "Sam Cowley, manager, was on alert night and day during the football season looking after the interests of the team. Every man on the squad testifies that Sam was constantly on the job, willing to do all he could to make things pleasant for them and at the same time looking after the details of team management in a competent and dependable manner." Sam was also a member of the Theta Beta Chapter of the Sigma Chi Fraternity.

During the summers, Sam traveled for the Union Knitting Mills of Logan selling knitted goods. This gave him opportunities to engage people in gospel conversations.

An honor graduate in 1923 with a Bachelor's degree, he made his way to Washington, DC for further studies at George Washington University Law School. In Washington he was employed as a private secretary to Brossard, a member of the United States Tariff Commission. Brossard also was president of the Washington, DC, Branch of the Church. Sam also worked at Woodward and Lothrups department store to earn money for his law education. In the summer of 1925 he worked for the U.S. Census Bureau.

Sam passed the bar exam in December, 1928, and received his LLB law degree in the spring of 1929 (SPC, 46-50).

Sam Cowley circa 1934

2

Sam Joins the FBI

Cowley received an appointment as a special agent for the FBI at an annual salary of $2,900 for a life of hard work, excitement, and undeniable fascination.

Ironically, Sam, an offspring of a plural marriage, was received with open arms by the very government that worked so desperately to suppress the practice.

The Bureau was not taking on any weaklings. That first year as special agent is designed to show up the soft spots. On April 3, 1929, less than a month after graduating from the Division Training School, Cowley was sent to Los Angeles for a grueling eight-month assignment where he dealt with everything from bankruptcy to copyright infringement. Hoover described Sam as "the sort of man who never could be found in the limelight, and his excellence was his intelligent persistence and his thoroughness at doing what ought to be done. I never had to check a job done by Cowley" (SPC, 184).

"Sam had true courage. He was a plain, direct, devout man with the simplicity of true worth, honor, and dignity. His whole life was based on simple faith and determination to do his duty. What was necessary to do was done with dignity. There was no pretense in Sam. He knew no honest labor as beneath his dignity. He worked to achieve his education. We soon found out that Cowley was a man who turned out a large volume of work and who accepted responsibility and asked for more. His attitude was commendable, his loyalty beyond question, and his personal habits were above reproach" (Hoover, Marriott Letter).

It was during his service in Los Angeles that Sam met a lovely young woman named Lavon Chipman, a native of American Fork, Utah, and a member of one of the pioneer families who settled there.

Four months later they were married in the St. George, Utah, Temple—sealing their marriage for time and eternity in true Latter-day Saint fashion. Two sons were born to this union: John Foss, on 25 August, 1931, and Samuel Jr. on 29 March, 1934.

John Foss (left), Sam Jr., mother Lavon Chipman Cowley

In due course, Sam was stationed in Salt Lake City; Detroit; Chicago; Butte, Montana; and finally in Washington, DC, where he performed general investigative duties. While in Washington, Cowley found time to serve in the Washington, DC, Branch of the Church; he taught the Gospel Doctrine class in Sunday School. According to Hoover, "Sam's attitude and bearing were those of a man whose faith was rooted in certain basic certainties and who knew that results were beyond human responsibility and power. His was the calm of a man who did his best and left the final decision to a Higher Power" (Hoover, Marriott Letter).

In October, 1932, Sam was named supervisor of the Kidnap Desk. This position made Sam an integral part of the Lindbergh case.

Sam soon rose to the rank of Inspector, and was assigned to work closely with Assistant Director Harold Nathan.

Once when Sam received a salary raise, he told J. Edgar Hoover, "I appreciate this advancement . . . but more so, because of the fact that it indicates to me that you have seen fit to place additional responsibility and confidence in me. I hope that you will not be disappointed in my efforts to contribute to the splendid work being performed . . . I am enjoying more than I can express my work here . . . the more responsibility, the more I enjoy it" (Hoover, Marriott letter, 2). Sam was quickly becoming one of Hoover's most capable and trusted agents.

Hoover himself had joined the Justice Department in 1917, shortly after graduating from George Washington University Law School. His first assignment was to oversee enemy alien operations during World War I. He also assisted in the General Intelligence Division under Attorney General A. Mitchell Palmer, investigating suspected anarchists and communists. Hoover was eventually promoted to be the assistant to Director William J. Burns, who had previously run his own detective agency. When President Calvin Coolidge succeeded President Warren G. Harding in 1923, he appointed Harlan F. Stone to be the attorney general. Stone appointed Hoover as the director of the FBI on May 10, 1924.

By inclination and training, Hoover embodied the Progressive Tradition. His appointment ensured that the Bureau would keep that tradition alive.

By the end of the decade, special agent training was institutionalized, the field office inspection system was solidly in place, and the National Division of Identification and Information was collecting and compiling uniform crime statistics for the entire United States. Studies were underway that would lead to the creation of the technical laboratory and uniform crime reports.

When Hoover took over, the Bureau had 440 special agents working in nine field offices. By the beginning of the next decade, there were thirty field offices. Hoover instigated the uniform performance appraisal system for agent promotion and abandoned the seniority rule.

Hoover realized that public support was needed for the Bureau to function productively. In 1925, Attorney General Stone said, "The agents of the (FBI) have been impressed with the fact that the real problem of law enforcement is in trying to obtain the cooperation and sympathy of the public, and that they cannot hope to get such cooperation until they themselves merit the respect of the public" (fbi.com, Early Years).

Regular inspections of the field office operations were scheduled. Formal training for new agents was established in early 1928. All new agents were required to be between 25 and 35 years of age and have law or accounting degrees.

In Hoover's initial running of the Bureau, one of his goals was to establish an identification office, which would track criminals by means of identification records. Matching fingerprints was seen as the most accurate method to accomplish this. The forerunner to this facility was the Bureau of Criminal Identification, established in the Justice Department in 1905 to provide a centralized fingerprint reference collection.

In 1907, this database was moved to Leavenworth Prison in Kansas where it was staffed by inmates. But suspicion of this arrangement led the International Association of Chiefs of Police to create their own fingerprint collection. In 1924, Congress merged the two collections in Washington, DC, and placed the new unit under the FBI.

The depression of the 1930s brought in the so-called gangster era. This crime wave ran unchecked, but Hoover mounted an unrelenting fight against such criminals as 'Ma' Barker, 'Pretty Boy' Floyd, John Dillinger, and 'Baby Face' Nelson.

To increase public support for the fledgling agency, Hoover relied on newspapers, radio, and the motion picture industry to publicize the accomplishments of his agents in making his Bureau the premier law enforcement agency in America. In 1932, a novel research facility called the Technical Laboratory was established.

The kidnapping sprees and the interstate movements of high profile gangsters prompted Congress to enact tough legislation to combat these lawless activities. The Lindberg Law was passed in 1932 to help prevent kidnappings, a favorite crime of that period. In 1934, the Dyer Act gave the agents jurisdiction over auto theft and prostitution when state lines were crossed in committing such crimes. The agents were also given federal arrest powers and authorization to carry weapons.

After the passage of the Lindbergh Law, which made kidnapping a Federal crime, Assistant FBI Director Harold Nathan took to the field to assist the special agents in enforcing the new statute. Inspector Hugh Clegg moved up to become acting assistant director. Cowley, still a special agent, moved up to do Clegg's work. The fire of crime blazed higher, and Clegg went out to assist Nathan. Sam then advanced to the post of assistant director in charge of investigations.

In July of 1934, Sam was promoted to Inspector and was picked to head up the FBI's anti-gangster effort. By age 35, he had built a reputation for himself as one of Hoover's shining stars, a man with a "brilliant analytical mind, and a tireless work ethic" (nlcomf.com, 1).

Even though headquartered in Washington, DC, in 1934, Sam worked much of his time in Chicago studying Dillinger and reporting his recommendations directly to Hoover (SPC, 21-24).

3

THE DEMISE OF PRETTY BOY FLOYD

On the morning of June 17, 1933, a mass murder was committed in front of the Kansas City Union Railroad Station, killing four law officers and their prisoner. It came to be known as the Kansas City Massacre.

It was an ill-fated attempt by Charles Arthur 'Pretty-Boy' Floyd, along with two of his henchmen, Vernon Miller and Adam Richetti, to free their friend, Frank Nash. Nash was in the custody of Federal agents who were returning him to Leavenworth Prison, Kansas, from which he had escaped October 19, 1930. Nash had been serving a 25-year sentence for assaulting a postal worker.

Sam was soon assigned investigative responsibilities for trailing Floyd and his two accomplices.

Nash's criminal record reached back to 1913 when he was sentenced to life at the Oklahoma State Prison in McAlester for murder. He was pardoned in 1920 and given a 25-year sentence at the same penitentiary for burglary with explosives, then later pardoned for that crime. On March 3, 1924, Nash began a 25-year sentence at Leavenworth for assaulting a mailroom custodian.

The FBI launched an intense search for Nash that spanned the entire United States and parts of Canada. Evidence gathered by Bureau agents indicated that Nash had assisted in the escape of seven prisoners from Leavenworth on December 11, 1931. The investigation also disclosed Nash's close association with Francis L. Keating, Thomas Holden, and several other well-known gunmen who had participated in a number of bank robberies throughout the Midwest. Keating and Holden were apprehended by FBI agents on July 7, 1932, in Kansas City, Missouri. Information gained as a result of the apprehension of the two indicated that Nash's underworld contacts were affording him protection in Hot Springs, Arkansas.

Based on such information, two FBI men—Frank Smith and Joseph Lackey—along with McAlester, Oklahoma Police Chief, Otto Reed, located and cornered Nash in a Hot Springs store. On June 16, 1933, the lawmen drove Nash to Ft. Smith, Arkansas, where they caught a train at 8:30 that evening bound for Kansas City. It was due at the Union Station at 7:15 the next morning. Before pulling out, the lawmen made arrangements for R. E. Vetterli, Special Agent in Charge of the Kansas City field office, to meet them at the Union Station. Nash was to be driven by car from Kansas City to Leavenworth.

On their way to Kansas City, Floyd and Richetti had been detained at Bolivar, Missouri, early on the morning of the 16th when their car was disabled. While the two waited in a local garage for repairs, Sheriff Jack Killingsworth entered the building. Richetti recognized the sheriff and seized a machine gun, forcing the lawman and the garage attendants against the wall. Floyd drew two .45 caliber automatic pistols and ordered all parties to remain motionless.

Floyd and Richetti then transferred their arsenal to another automobile and ordered Sheriff Killingsworth inside the car. They drove to Deepwater, Missouri, abandoned that car, and commandeered another. After releasing the sheriff, they drove on to Kansas City, arriving about 10 p.m. Upon arriving there,

Floyd and Richetti abandoned that car and stole another, where they transferred their baggage and firearms. They met up with Vernon Miller and went with him to his home, where he told them of his plan to free Nash.

Early the next morning, Miller, Floyd, and Richetti drove to the Union Station in a Chevrolet sedan. There they took up their positions to await the arrival of Nash and his captors.

When the train arrived in Kansas City, Agent Lackey went to the loading platform, leaving Agent Smith, Chief Reed, and Nash in a stateroom aboard the train. On the platform, Lackey was met by Special Agent Vetterli, who was accompanied by Special Agent R. J. Caffrey and Officers W. J. Grooms and Frank Hermanson of the Kansas City Police Department. These men surveyed the area surrounding the platform and saw nothing that aroused their suspicion. Vetterli advised Lackey that he and Caffrey had brought two cars to the station and that the cars were parked immediately outside.

Lackey returned to the train. Accompanied by Chief Reed, Agents Vetterli, Caffrey, and Smith, and Officers Hermanson and Grooms, Lackey proceeded through the Union Station lobby. At the time, both Lackey and Reed were armed with shotguns. The other officers carried pistols. Nash walked handcuffed through Union Station, escorted by the officers. Upon exiting the station, the lawmen took their captive to Caffrey's Chevrolet, parked directly in front of the station's east entrance.

Caffrey unlocked the door on the passenger side of the Chevrolet. When the door was open, Nash started to climb into the rear seat. Lackey told him to get into the front seat. Lackey then climbed into the back of the car directly behind the driver's seat. Smith sat beside him in the center of the back seat, and Chief Reed jammed himself in beside Smith in the right rear seat. At this point, Caffrey walked around the car to get into the driver's seat through the left door. Vetterli stood with Hermanson and Grooms at the right side near the front of the car. A green Plymouth was parked about six feet away on the right side of Caffrey's car. Suddenly, Lackey saw two men run from behind the Plymouth. He noticed that both were armed. At least one of them had a machine gun. Before Lackey had a chance to warn his fellow officers, one of the gunmen shouted, "Let 'em have it!"

At this point, from a distance of about 15 feet diagonally to the right of Caffrey's car, someone who was crouched behind the radiator of another car opened fire. Officers Grooms and Hermanson were shot dead and fell immediately to the ground. Vetterli, who was standing beside them, was shot in the left arm and dropped to the ground. As he scrambled to the left side of the car to join Caffrey, who had not yet entered the driver's seat, Vetterli saw Caffrey fall to the ground, fatally wounded in the head.

Inside the car, Nash and Chief Reed were killed by bullets from the hoodlums' guns. Agents Lackey and Smith were able to survive the massacre by falling forward in the back seat. Lackey was struck and seriously wounded by three bullets. Smith escaped unscathed.

The gunmen rushed to the lawmen's car and looking inside, one of them remarked, "They're all dead. Let's get out of here." With that they raced toward a dark-colored Chevrolet. Just then several Kansas City policemen came running out of the station, drawn by the gunfire. They shot in the direction of Floyd, who slumped briefly but continued to run toward the getaway car. The killers piled into the Chevrolet and with squealing tires roared westward out of the parking lot and disappeared.

The three survivors—Smith, Lackey, and Vetterli—reported that the assault lasted about thirty seconds. From their account, it was apparent that the two Kansas City policemen were killed immediately, followed seconds later by Nash and Chief Reed, then by Caffrey, who was taken to a hospital and pronounced dead on arrival.

Sam Cowley immediately initiated an investigation to identify and apprehend the gunmen. He headed for the Midwest. Evidence showed that the scheme was carried out by Miller, Richetti, and Floyd. A latent fingerprint on beer bottles in Miller's home identified Adam Richetti, linking him to the suspects. Latent fingerprint identification was then state-of-the-art technology; using the silver nitrate method, investigators could raise incriminating prints from surfaces that couldn't be dusted. Unseen fingerprints contain perspiration which is full of sodium chloride, a common table salt. By painting the ransom notes with a silver nitrate solution, the salty perspiration reacted chemically to form silver chloride, which is visible to the naked eye (fbi.org, Forensics First).

Using this evidence, Cowley organized a nationwide search for the 29-year-old Floyd, who had a long history of breaking the law (fbi.org, Kansas City Massacre).

4
THE NET IS CLOSING

After fleeing Kansas City, Floyd and Richetti eventually made their way back to Toledo, where they met Beulah Baird and her sister, Rose. In October, 1933, the four went to Buffalo, New York, where they rented an apartment. Floyd and Beulah adopted the alias 'Mr. and Mrs. George Sanders,' and Richetti and Rose were known as 'Mr. and Mrs. Ed Brennan.'

The two couples seldom left their apartment and only then for groceries. Floyd paced the floor constantly, disturbing some of the building's occupants. Finally, after a year, in October, 1934, Rose bought a Ford sedan and they left for Oklahoma. Their car was damaged in a minor one-car accident in Wellsville, Ohio. Floyd removed the weapons from the car and Beulah and Rose took it to a repair shop while Floyd and Richetti lingered just outside of town.

Wellsville Police Chief J. H. Fultz got wind of the two men loitering near town and upon investigation found them hiding in a secluded wooded area. As guns blazed, Fultz wounded Floyd, but he and Richetti managed to avoid capture.

Cowley had been closely monitoring developments in the Floyd case ever since the Kansas City Massacre. He sent a squad of Federal agents to aid in the manhunt for Floyd. They were joined by four East Liverpool, Ohio policemen, led by Chief Hugh McDermot. As they patrolled a road south of Clarkson, they noticed a car move rapidly from behind a corn crib on a nearby farm. They stopped their cars to question the occupants of the mysterious car from the corn crib. The law officers immediately recognized Floyd when he jumped from the car with a .45-caliber automatic pistol in his hand.

As a gun battle ensued, Floyd cried, "I'm done for, you've hit me twice" (SPC, 180). They removed the pistol from his hand and seized a second that he was carrying in his belt. Two agents left to summon an ambulance to take Floyd to a hospital. The action was witnessed by several local citizens, including the farm owner where the shooting occurred. Floyd died a few minutes after he was shot, before medical help could arrive. Agents found a watch fob with 10 notches reportedly carved by Floyd, indicating the number of persons he had killed.

Rose and Beulah Baird, waiting for their car to be repaired, found out that Floyd had been killed and Richetti had been arrested elsewhere. They left immediately for Sallisaw, Oklahoma, and attended the funeral for Charles 'Pretty Boy' Floyd.

Floyd had been arrested on numerous occasions for almost a decade—the first time by St Louis police in September, 1925, for highway robbery. He pleaded guilty to that charge on December 8, 1925, was sentenced to the state prison at Jefferson City, Missouri, and was released almost three-and-a-half years later in March, 1929. One day later he was arrested in Kansas City for vagrancy and suspicion of highway robbery. He was again sent to prison and released in May, 1930. Floyd was arrested by the Toledo, Ohio police on a bank robbery charge and sentenced in November to 12-15 years in the Ohio State Penitentiary. Floyd escaped en route to the prison and was a fugitive from justice when he became involved in the Kansas City Massacre in the summer of 1933.

One of Floyd's henchmen in the Kansas City Massacre, Vernon C. Miller, grew up in South Dakota. He enlisted in the Army in WWI and trained extensively as a machine gunner. He bragged about his war heroism when he returned from the front to Huron, South Dakota. He told city officials he was a crack shot and was appointed to the local police force in 1920. Two years later he was elected sheriff and was re-nominated for the position. But before the election, he disappeared into a life of crime.

Miller's criminal record indicated that he had been arrested on April 4, 1923 and was sentenced to 2-to-10 years and charged a $5,200 fine for embezzling public funds. In October, 1925, he was indicted in Federal Court in Sioux Falls, South Dakota, for violating the national Prohibition Act. The case was *nole prosequi* (the prosecutor will proceed no further) in January of 1931. Miller then moved to St Paul, Minnesota, and on to Chicago where he began his association with underworld gangs. Miller was reported to have been a hired gunman for Louis Buchalter early in his crime career.

Following the Kansas City Massacre, Miller went to Chicago, accompanied by a girlfriend, Vivian Mathias, in June, 1933. He hid out there temporarily with a member of the Barker-Karpis gang. By October, 1933, the FBI had discovered that Miller was in Chicago and hiding in Vivian's apartment. The next day he eluded a trap but Vivian was taken into custody and later pleaded guilty to harboring Miller.

Miller was involved in a fight with a henchman of Lonnie Zwillman, head of New Jersey's underworld mob, in Newark. During the argument, Miller killed the henchman. Miller was slain in retaliation.

Adam C. Richetti, another of Floyd's henchmen in the Kansas City Massacre, began his criminal career with an arrest in Hammond, Indiana, in August, 1928, for a holdup. Sentenced to 1-10 years in the state reformatory at Pendleton, he was paroled and later released from parole in September, 1931. His next run-in with the law occurred in March, 1932, for a Sulpher, Oklahoma bank robbery. This time he was confined in the State Penitentiary at McAlester from April to August, 1932, when he was released on bond, which he promptly jumped. Three years later, Richetti was nabbed for bond jumping and an Oklahoma robbery. He was returned to Kansas City in March, 1935. After finding Richetti guilty on four counts of murder, the jury recommended death. Richetti was sentenced to be hanged. He appealed, claiming insanity, but his conviction was upheld by the Missouri Supreme Court. He was found sane, and sentenced to die in the Missouri gas chamber in Jefferson City. He was executed October 7, 1938.

Four nameless individuals who had assisted in the attempt to free Nash at the Kansas City Union Station were tried and found guilty of causing the escape of a federal prisoner from custody. Each was sentenced to two years in a Federal Prison and fined $10,000—the maximum penalty under the law.

5

THE BARKER-KARPIS KIDNAPPINGS

As Cowley was on his way to the Midwest to help round up the gang involved in the Kansas City Massacre, Mrs. Berry V. Stoll, 26, of Louisville, Kentucky, was kidnapped. Cowley temporarily turned his attention to the hunt for Thomas H. Robinson, Jr., suspected of committing the crime. Mrs. Stoll was the daughter-in-law of wealthy oilman Charles C. Stoll. The kidnapper had demanded $50,000 ransom. After six days the ransom was paid and Mrs. Stoll was released in Indianapolis, Indiana. Cowley and Purvis continued searching for suspected kidnapper Robinson, a native of Nashville, Tennessee.

Robinson was captured 18 months later in California, convicted, and sentenced to life at Alcatraz. It was common gossip that he may have been framed by the victim. He was eventually granted a new trial in 1943, convicted again, and sentenced to death. President Harry S Truman commuted his sentence to life in prison.

For Cowley, the kidnapping wave was just getting started. On a warm June evening in 1933, William Hamm, a St Paul, Minnesota brewer, was snatched and held for $100,000 ransom. The Hamm case has all the elements of an old gangster flick—a gang of criminals and a high profile kidnapping.

Hamm had just left his office building when he was nabbed by four shadowy figures and shoved into the back seat of an automobile. What Hamm didn't realized was that he had just been kidnapped by members of the Barker-Karpis gang. Hamm was driven to Wisconsin, where he was forced to sign four ransom notes. Then he was moved to a gang hideout in Bensenville, Illinois, where he was held captive until the ransom money was paid.

Once the money had changed hands, Hamm was released near Wyoming, Minnesota. The plan appeared to have been pulled off without a hitch. Members of the Barker-Karpis gang were the leading suspects in the case, but the Bureau had few clues. Again, Sam Cowley was assigned to locate another ruthless gang.

The band consisted of Kate (Ma), and her sons: Arthur (Dock), Fred (Freddie), Herman, Lloyd, and Alvin Karpis. While agents were speedily tracking down leads and gathering evidence, the gang slipped into St. Paul and robbed $30,000 from a messenger of a meat packing firm, right on the front steps of the main post office, killing a police officer during the course of the crime.

The entire gang then traveled to Reno, Nevada, to launder their ill-gotten loot through Ma's underworld connections. The ransom money was never found. By September 6, three months after the Hamm kidnapping, the FBI was heavily involved in the case. Alvin Karpis, Dock Barker, Charles Fitzgerald, and the rest of the gang had gotten away but left their fingerprints behind, all over the ransom notes.

In the Hamm kidnapping case, investigators used latent fingerprint identification successfully for the first time to raise incriminating prints from surfaces that couldn't be dusted. This gave them hard evidence that the Barker-Karpis bunch was behind the crime. Most of the FBI's attention was focused on Alvin Karpis, so the man hunt for him went forward in full force.

"Alvin Karpis (born Karpacvis) wanted everything in life without working for it," Hoover wrote in *Persons in Hiding*. "His descent to ratdom began in 1930 when he joined up with Fred Barker and went into training at Ma's crime school in Joplin, Missouri" (*Persons in Hiding*, 42). Karpis and Freddie had met in prison and were released about the same time. Alvin came into the forefront driving the kidnap getaway car, knocking victims unconscious, guarding hideouts, and purchasing the gang's supplies. Working under Ma, Karpis became kill-crazy to the extent that his own gang members feared him, often referring to him as 'Old Creepy.'

Alvin's eyes were frigid and aged, according to Hoover's account. "They were penetrating as if peering out from a dark corner. His mouth was a cruel thin slice. His cheeks were those of an old man—drooped and jowled. He used foul language beyond reason. Cold as ice, he possessed a cruel, sadistic sense of humor."

Alvin finally broke one of Ma's cardinal rules. He got drunk and met Dolores Delaney, a 16-year-old bar-hopping cop-hater. He took her for his woman, for she was the type who would follow her man to hell. Dolores appeared to be naive and pretended not to know Alvin was a crook. She even played dumb when he was absent from their apartment while the newspapers blared that William Hamm had been kidnapped and was being held for $100,000 ransom.

When police raided their apartment, Karpis made his escape, but left pregnant Dolores behind. Ever the forgiving wife, Dolores named her baby Raymond Alvin Karpacvis, and immediately placed him with his grandparents, John and Anna Karpacvis.

Dolores pleaded guilty to harboring Karpis and went to prison for five years. Meanwhile, Karpis was on the run from state to state, always a step ahead of his pursuers. He was finally traced to an apartment in New Orleans. Hoover joined the squad who traveled there to apprehend the wary Karpis. As the agents approached the front door, Karpis was coming out. Taken by surprise, he was nabbed without incident. At last, one of America's worst criminals was in custody. He was tried and convicted for the kidnapping of William Hamm and sentenced to Alcatraz for life.

While in prison, he wrote a letter to Dolores:

> I suppose now you realize that all that glitters is not gold, In other words, when you are released from prison, stay on the straight and narrow path. You may think that rather strange coming from me, but I should know.

"Ma Barker had the most vicious, dangerous and resourceful criminal brain of the 1930s," Hoover wrote. "Her murderous satellites called her 'Mother Barker' and she headed what we know as the Barker-Karpis gang of hoodlums, highwaymen and kidnappers" (*Persons in Hiding*, 9).

In her 60-some years, she became a monument to the evils of parental indulgence. Of her four sons, one became a mail robber, another a holdup man, and the remaining pair were highwaymen, kidnappers, and wanton murderers. To a great extent their criminal careers were directly traceable to their mother. She pampered them like a young parent with her first baby, and they obeyed her as implicitly as the thoroughly disciplined children of a Puritan.

Ma Barker had no counterpart as a parent in ruthlessness or desperation. Her wild antipathy for any interference in the wayward lives of her sons not only led to a life of crime for her children, but made her an arch-criminal, Hoover continued.

Her childhood on a Missouri farm was made up of church, Sunday school, picnics, hayrides, candy pulls, and the little red schoolhouse. She was christened Arizona Clark, but soon picked up the nickname 'Kate.' She met a young farm laborer, George Barker. They were married when Kate was barely out of her teens. She was known as a good wife, devoted to the church, a fair housekeeper, and averse to back fence gossip. George was a mild, ineffective, quiet man who was somewhat bewildered by his wife. When he attempted to give guidance to his growing boys who were his pride and joy, Kate made sure that no one but herself would ever be their mentor.

George finally drifted away from the family, taking odd jobs and wondering why his good boys were going astray. Ma soon took up with a new male companion, Arthur Dunlop, a nondescript simpleton who mainly used Ma as his meal ticket (*Persons in Hiding*, 23).

Whenever her boys got into any kind of trouble, Ma rushed to their rescue, pleading with the police to go easy on them, paying for things they stole or for damage they caused in their steady climb up the criminal ladder. She taught them how to lie for each other to avoid arrest for their shenanigans.

In a vain attempt to disguise the boys so they could evade detection, she arranged with Dr. Joseph P. Moran to surgically disfigure their fingertips enough to escape tracing. So the Devil Doctor to the underworld butchered the boys' fingers sans anesthetic. It was a brutal operation involving terrific pain. Ma nursed them through endless days of agony, partially subdued with morphine. Their suffering was in vain because when their digits healed, they showed the same fingerprint patterns as before the operations.

The Barker gang became more and more suspicious of Dunlop as the police informant who led to their capture and arrest. His body was found on the shore of a Minnesota lake.

Ma traveled under several aliases. She was known as Mrs. F. E. Gordon of Rockford, Illinois, Mrs. T. E. Anderson of

Chicago, and Mrs. A. S. Hunter—renting apartments with the best references, turning them into nests for her criminal brood.

Ma and her gang jumped on the kidnapping bandwagon in 1934; Edward Bremer, a St. Paul banker, was seized in January, 1934, by the Barker-Karpis gang and held for $200,000 ransom. His father, Edward Sr., was a personal friend and political donor to President Franklin D. Roosevelt. FDR spoke of the Bremer incident on one of his radio fireside chats, bringing public attention to the kidnapping.

The Lindbergh baby kidnapping two years before was still in the news. As a result of this crime, Congress made kidnapping a federal offense, bringing all the enforcement efforts of the FBI into play in every kidnapping case. Cowley was in charge of the FBI's kidnap desk in Washington, DC, and was heavily involved in the Lindbergh, Hamm, and Bremer cases. On payment of the ransom, Bremer was being returned from the hideout in Bensenville, Illinois, to Rochester, Minnesota, for his release. The gang stopped along the way to refuel their cars. Following various leads, FBI agents tracked down the gas station where the refueling took place. There they found several gasoline cans. One had Arthur 'Dock' Barker's fingerprint on it. This evidence linked the Barker-Karpis gang to Bremer's abduction.

Thus, for the first time, Ma Barker and her brood came under Federal jurisdiction. Ma was at the center of the kidnapping. She kept in contact with the gang members during the sending of ransom notes, and while making quick trips to and from their hideout. She also helped count the ransom money.

As the investigators continued to pore over the evidence, they nailed Dock for his role in the kidnapping. He was sent to Alcatraz Prison for life. Lloyd went to Leavenworth Federal Penitentiary for robbery of the U.S. mails. Herman teamed up with Ray Terrill and during a holdup in Newton, Kansas, Herman hit and killed a police officer with his car in an attempt to flee. But he beat the hangman by killing himself near Wichita, Kansas, where his body was found among roadside weeds.

That left Ma and Freddie. As the intense investigation continued in the early months of 1935, agents turned up a map that indicted Ma and Freddie Barker might be holed up near Ocala, Florida. A special squad was dispatched from Chicago to locate the house the Barkers were supposed to be living in. As the agents surrounded the house, the inspector in charge called for the Barkers to surrender.

Instead, the agents were met with heavy gunfire. Ma blasted from an upstairs window with a submachine gun and Freddie fired a rifle from downstairs. When the shooting ceased, agents entered the house to find Freddie dead, with his rifle clutched in his hands. Ma also died, with her machine gun lying cross her body. Ma and Freddie were buried in Welch, Oklahoma, alongside the remains of Herman.

Along with the squad inspector who led the raid, Hoover credited Sam Cowley for laying the ground work for the gang's destruction and successfully closing the final chapter of the Barker-Karpis reign of terror (*Persons in Hiding*, 114).

With Lloyd in Leavenworth, Dock and Karpis sentenced to life in Alcatraz, Herman, Freddie, and Ma dead, father George Barker carried on with his job as handyman at a local filling station, tying to forget all that had befallen his family.

6
THE HUNT FOR DILLINGER

John Dillinger was a brutal thief and a cold-blooded murderer. From September, 1933, to July, 1934, he and his gang terrorized the Midwest—killing ten men and wounding seven others. He robbed banks and police arsenals, and he staged three jailbreaks, killing a sheriff during one and wounding two guards during another. Dillinger was Public Enemy No. 1, and Hoover made the search for him top priority.

Dillinger was born June 22, 1903, in Indianapolis, Indiana. His mother died when he was only three years old. John's father was a harsh, repressive disciplinarian, yet at times permissive. John's father remarried six years later, and John always resented his stepmother.

In adolescence, the flaws in his bewildering personality became evident, and he was frequently in trouble.

Finally, Dillinger quit school and went to work in a machine shop in Indianapolis. Although intelligent and a good worker, he was soon bored and often stayed out all night. His father gave up his grocery business and moved the family to a farm near Mooresville, hoping young John would find a better life there. John's father felt the temptations of the big city were corrupting his teenage son. John reacted no better to rural life than he had in the city and soon began to run wild again. A break with his father and trouble with the law for auto theft led John to enlist in the Navy. There he soon got into trouble and deserted his ship when it docked in Boston.

Returning home to Mooresville, he married 16-year-old Beryl Hovius in 1924. Sizzling dreams of bright lights and excitement led the newlyweds to Indianapolis. Dillinger had no luck finding work in the city, so he joined forces with the town pool shark, Ed Singleton, in his search for easy money. In their first attempt at crime, they tried to rob a Mooresville grocery store but were quickly apprehended. Singleton pleaded not guilty, stood trial, and was convicted and given a two-year sentence. Dillinger followed his father's advice and confessed. He was convicted of assault and battery, with intent to rob and conspiracy to commit a felony. He received joint sentences of 2-to-14 years and 10-to-20 years in the Indiana State Penitentiary. Stunned by the harsh sentence, Dillinger became a tortured and bitter man while in prison.

He was paroled in May, 1933, and soon robbed a bank in Bluffton, Ohio. He was caught by Dayton police in September and lodged in the Lima jail to await trial. Dillinger bragged that no jail could hold him. While frisking Dillinger, the Lima police found a document that seemed to be a plan for a prison break, but John denied knowledge of any such plan. Four days later, using that very plan, eight of Dillinger's friends escaped from the Indiana State Prison using shotguns and rifles which had been smuggled into their cells. During the escape, they shot two guards. Three of the escaped prisoners, along with a parolee from the same prison, showed up at the Lima jail, telling the sheriff they had come to return Dillinger to the state prison for parole violations. When Sheriff Jess Sarber asked for their credentials, they pulled guns and shot him. With Dillinger freed, they locked the sheriff's wife and a deputy in a cell and made their getaway, leaving Sarber to die on the floor.

Although none of these men had violated any Federal law, FBI assistance was requested in identifying and locating the criminals. The four were identified as Harry Pierpont, Russell Clark, Charles Makley, and Harry Copeland. Their fingerprint cards in the FBI identification division were flagged with red tags, indicating that they were wanted men. The gang pulled several bank robberies as they moved across Indiana. They plundered police arsenals at Auburn and Peru, stealing machine guns, rifles, revolvers, a quantity of ammunition, and several bulletproof vests.

On December 14, John Hamilton, a Dillinger gang member, shot and killed a police detective in Chicago. A month later the gang robbed the First National Bank of East Chicago, Indiana, killing a police officer. The Dillinger gang then fled to Arizona. There on January 23, 1934, a fire broke out in the hotel where Clark and Makley were hiding under assumed names. Responding to the fire, police recognized the men from photos and arrested them, as well as Dillinger and Pierpont. In the course of a search of their hotel rooms, police seized Thompson submachine guns, modified Winchester rifles, bulletproof vests, and more than $25,000 in cash—part of the East Chicago robbery loot. During his extradition, John became the first fugitive to be flown in an airplane.

Dillinger was returned to Indiana, where he was jailed to await trial for the murder of the East Chicago policeman. Authorities boasted that their Crown Point jail was escape-proof. But on March 3, Dillinger held the guards at bay with what he later claimed was a wooden gun he had whittled and covered with black shoe polish. He grabbed two machineguns, locked up the guards and a trustee, and fled in a stolen car. It was then Dillinger made the mistake that would cost him his life. He stole Sheriff Hoolley's Ford V-8 and drove it across the Indiana-Illinois state line, heading to Chicago. He thus violated the National Motor Vehicle Theft Act, which made it a Federal crime to drive a stolen car across a state line.

As soon as the federal grand jury in Chicago indicted Dillinger, Cowley launched a nationwide manhunt for him. Meanwhile, Pierpont, Makley, and Clark were returned to Ohio and convicted of the murder of Sheriff Sarber in Lima. Pierpont and Makley were sentence to death, and Clark to life. But during an escape attempt, Makley was killed and Pierpont was wounded. A month later, Pierpont had recovered sufficiently to be executed.

In Chicago, Dillinger joined up with his girlfriend, Evelyn Frechette. The two traveled to St. Paul, Minnesota, where they teamed up with Homer Van Meter, Eddie Green, and Tommy Carroll. It was here that Dillinger first met Lester Gillis, aka George 'Baby Face' Nelson.

Dillinger and Evelyn listed themselves as Mr. and Mrs. Hellman, appropriately enough. By this time most of the Dillinger gang was either jailed or dead, so Dillinger invited Nelson to join his gang and move into robbing banks big time.

Dillinger didn't care much for Nelson's maniacal tendencies nor his uncontrollable temper. But the two continued as a team, and went on a gigantic bank-robbing spree, netting thousands of dollars.

On March 30, 1934, the manager of the Lincoln Court Apartments in St. Paul became suspicious of some of his tenants. He notified police, and soon FBI agents knocked at the door of one of the apartments. Evelyn Frechette opened the door, then quickly slammed it shut. Agents called for backup and surrounded the apartment building. Agents saw a man enter a hallway near the Hellman apartment. When they questioned him they learned that he was Homer Van Meter. He drew a gun. Shots were fired, and Van Meter fled the building and forced a truck driver at gunpoint to drive him to Eddie Green's apartment. Suddenly, the door of the Hellman apartment opened and the muzzle of a machine gun began spraying lead in the hallway. Under cover of the shooting, Dillinger and Evelyn fled through a back door. They drove to Green's apartment where Dillinger was treated for a bullet wound sustained in the escape from their apartment.

At the Lincoln Court apartments, the FBI found a Thompson submachine gun with the stock removed, two automatic rifles, a .38 caliber automatic pistol with a 20-shot clip, and two bulletproof vests. Across town other agents located one of Eddie Green's hideouts where he and Bessie Skinner had been living as Mr. and Mrs. Stephens. Green was located on April 3. He attempted to draw his gun but was shot by agents and died in a local hospital eight days later.

Dillinger and Evelyn fled to Mooresville, where they stayed with his father and half-brother until his wounds healed. Then Frechette went to Chicago to visit a friend and was there arrested by the FBI. She was returned to St. Paul for trial on conspiracy to harbor a fugitive. She was convicted, fined $1,000, and sentenced to two years in prison. Bessie Skinner, Eddie Green's girlfriend, got 15 months on the same charge. Meanwhile, Dillinger and Van Meter robbed a police station of guns and bulletproof vests in Warsaw, Indiana. Dillinger then stayed for a while in Upper Michigan, departing just ahead of a squad of FBI agents who had been dispatched there to apprehend him. Then, the Bureau received a tip that there had been a sudden influx of rather suspicious guests at the summer resort of Little Bohemia Lodge, about 50 miles north of Rhinelander, Wisconsin. The resort was usually vacant this time of year, and the presence of the gang members aroused the suspicion of the owner, who telephoned police. His message was relayed to the Chicago FBI field office (fbi.org, John Dillinger). From their descriptions, one of them was thought to be Dillinger and another 'Baby Face' Nelson.

7
THE RHINELANDER RENDEZVOUS

On April 22, agents from throughout the Midwest were ordered to rendezvous at Rhinelander where Purvis set up a temporary field office. He briefed the task force of 30 agents on his ill-conceived plan to trap Dillinger and Nelson.

During the dark early morning hours of April 23, agents set out in cars for Little Bohemia. When the Federal posse arrived at the lodge, barking dogs alerted the gangsters, and as the agents surrounded the building, gunfire erupted from the rooftop.

Three men hurried from the lodge, jumped into a car and drove away from the building. Purvis ordered them to stop, but they ignored the warning and continued down the driveway. Agents opened fire, killing the driver and injuring the two passengers. Investigation soon revealed that the men were not connected with the gangsters but were innocent patrons of the lodge restaurant just leaving for home.

Dillinger and Nelson escaped out the back door and fled into the woods as the agents entered the building. Helen was left behind and arrested for harboring a fugitive. Nelson made his way to a farmhouse belonging to Mr. and Mrs. Alvin Koerner. Taking them hostage, he made a getaway with them in their family car. Special Agents W. Carter Baum and J.C. Newman, along with Carl Christensen, a local constable, found Nelson in the car holding the Koerners. Nelson quickly shot the three lawmen, killing Baum and severely wounding Newman and Christensen.

Petitions circulated quickly in the area around Little Bohemia calling for the suspension of Melvin Purvis, accused of acting with "wanton recklessness and disregard of human life," in the shooting of the three innocent patrons of the lodge.

This horrendous chapter in history was in the midst of America's worst economic depression, which adversely touched nearly everyone in the country. Dillinger, in a perverse way, was one of the few individuals succeeding in these very hard times. He was getting money, and he was getting away—all the while gaining considerable public acclaim—even approval in some quarters. He was viewed by many as a sort of Robin Hood. This was not helping the Bureau succeed in its greatest challenge to date.

Humiliated by the Little Bohemia fiasco, J. Edgar Hoover was furious that Purvis and his agents had broken a cardinal rule—that FBI operations be well planned and competently carried out to earn the confidence and respect of a worried nation. Hoover needed to get Dillinger and Nelson, so he adopted new measures.

"I called Sam Cowley into my office," Hoover said. "By this time I knew he was one of our most determined and capable men, but I think my choice was based on something more than that. To me, Dillinger and his gang were the personification of evil. Sam was one of the finest characters I had ever known. I think that, unconsciously, perhaps, I was trying to oppose this vile personification of evil with the highest example of good it had been my pleasure to know" (*Deseret News Magazine*).

Hoover instructed Sam, now an inspector with a direct line to the director, to go to Chicago and put together a task force to track down Dillinger wherever the trail led. Hoover gave him the green light and assured him that all the Bureau's resources were at his disposal: "'Sam, stay on Dillinger,' I told him. 'Follow the trail wherever it takes you. Find everyone who was ever connected with his gang, no matter how remotely. Take Dillinger alive if you can, but take him. And always protect yourself'" (SPC, 188).

On July 1, 1934, Inspector Cowley went to Chicago to head up the Dillinger Squad, reporting directly to Hoover. Cowley knew that he had received an assignment that would never be changed until it was fulfilled. He and Hoover and no one else in America, except agents who would be used in this case, knew that Dillinger was Cowley's quarry. Special Agent Purvis remained in charge of the Chicago field office and all other criminal matters falling within the jurisdiction of that office.

The newly arrived Cowley contrasted sharply with Purvis. Purvis was small, excitable, impulsive, and quick. Cowley was careful, calm, analytical, somber; moving deliberately with sound judgment. He was a serious, dedicated man, and he drove the men on the Dillinger detail so relentlessly that some complained. But they soon realized that Cowley drove himself even harder. Hoover said of Sam's work ethic that he was usually the first into the office and the last to leave.

Sam picked 30 agents for his Dillinger Squad. They worked quietly from the back rooms of the Chicago office while Agent Purvis with his 25 men carried on as usual in the front rooms. Cowley's squad worked behind unmarked doors with unlisted telephones.

Two East Chicago, Indiana policemen, Captain Timothy O'Neill and Sergeant Martin Zarkovich, offered to cooperate with the agents in the final days of the hunt for Dillinger. Their fellow officer, Captain William Patrick O'Malley, had been slain by Dillinger in an East Chicago robbery, and they were there to avenge his death.

To Zarkovich, the trailing of Dillinger was a blood feud. He wanted to hang John Dillinger by the heels because of the bitterness he felt towards the outlaw for killing Capt. O'Malley, who was Zarkovich's commanding officer.

The pair had spent weeks making contacts and seeking someone who could tell them something definite about John Dillinger and his whereabouts. They had followed myriad blind clues and rumors to their end seeking that one vital spark of correct information. They'd tracked Dillinger from city to city and state to state. The search always brought them back to Chicago (SPC, 188, 189).

"I was assigned here by the (Bureau)," Cowley told a reporter, "and attached to the Chicago Branch to develop the Dillinger case. Police, particularly the two East Chicago men, were brought in with scores of agents from the (Bureau). We have one important confidential informant, and then hundreds upon hundreds of persons with and without vital information, all serving the government in its quest for the elusive Dillinger. All the information was studied, sorted, and checked by one man, J. Edgar Hoover, who constantly and always advised and directed every move. I was the officially assigned Dillinger man. Mr. Purvis was the Special Agent in charge of the Chicago office, where I finally came to know the quarry would be captured" (SPC, 188).

"The two East Chicago officers came in with their offers to cooperate in the final days of this hunt. Their offers were accepted willingly, as you may guess. They agreed with our theory that Dillinger was in Chicago; that all the recent reports of his death, his hideout in the Wisconsin north woods, his trips to Europe and to Los Angeles, were erroneous. Dillinger was in Chicago!" Cowley said.

"(The two East Chicago policemen) should be given the greatest of credit in this affair," Cowley declared. " They cooperated and worked with the (FBI) men in the field. They had already worked tirelessly as every man in the case had done. Checking false rumors, agreeing with the (Bureau) in that first conference that our knowledge and theirs dovetailed" (SPC, 188, 189).

In a fruitless attempt to disguise his appearance, on May 28 Dillinger enlisted the aid of Dr. Harold B. Cassedy, a back-alley quack, to alter his facial features and fingers in order to avoid recognition. To spare John the agonizing pain of the surgery, ether was used to put him to sleep. The outcome of the botched operation angered Dillinger. He was not satisfied with the results because most of his features had changed very little.

Cowley knew Dillinger was in Chicago. He had been seen in the city but at widely divergent points. Cowley feared identification would be difficult due to the surgical changes in the man's features: "We were sure we had the general neighborhood located. Our task was to narrow it down to a single street. The places in the district that would attract the man through his natural habits were watched and guarded in shifts. The little neighborhood movie house was one of them."

The pair of officers from East Chicago had found a person with actual knowledge of Dillinger's recent movements. This person could be expected to know Dillinger despite his surgical disguise. "The knowledge we obtained from this confidential informant was not positive," Cowley related. "It was to the effect that this man who strangely resembled the wanted bank robber and killer lived on North Halstead Street. His name was Jim Lawrence. He was a clerk at the Board of Trade."

Concerned for the safety of this man, Cowley said, "It is absurd to consider that such an informant cannot talk with absolute safety to us. The source of such information must be kept as inviolate as words spoken in a confessional. In fact, no reliable publication, knowing the facts, would reveal the name of such a person and so expose him to almost certain death at the hands of a hoodlum or some casual crank from the underworld, after he helped rid the country of a dangerous killer and robber" (SPC, 190).

8

THE WOMAN IN RED

Purvis received a tip that one Anna Sage might be willing to betray Dillinger. Sage was the madam of a Gary, Indiana, brothel. Her real name was Ana Cumpanas. She had come to America from Rumania in 1914. The Department of Labor, who handled deportation cases, classified her as undesirable due to the nature of her profession. Deportation proceedings had been started. Anna was willing to sell the FBI some information about Dillinger for a cash reward and their help in avoiding deportation. On July 21, 1934, she met with Cowley and Purvis, who promised her a reward if her information led to Dillinger's capture and told her even though they had no jurisdiction over the deportation proceedings, they would put in a good word for her, calling her cooperation to the attention of the Labor Department.

Anna was satisfied. She told the agents her girlfriend, Polly Hamilton, had visited her establishment with Dillinger, whom she recognized from a newspaper photo. Anna said that she, Polly, and Dillinger would be attending a movie the next evening at the Biograph or Marbro Theaters. She told them she would be in touch when she found out which theater they would attend. She agreed to wear a bright-colored dress, so they could easily pick her from the crowd at the theater. Agents visited both theaters—mapping exits, entrances, fire escapes, floor plans, streets, and alleys.

Sunday, July 22, was a hot, humid day in Chicago. Cowley, not knowing which theater Dillinger would attend, split up the task force with agents assigned to each theater. At 8:30 p.m. Anna, Polly, and Dillinger strolled into the Biograph to watch the film, *Manhattan Melodrama*, starring Clark Gable and Ronald Coleman. Anna did indeed wear a bright-colored dress. It was orange, but under the theater marquee lights, it was a vivid red, thus leading the Chicago press to dub her 'the woman in red.' Dillinger's bungled facelift had failed to hide his identity from the agents posted at the theater. They recognized him instantly from his photos they carried.

Purvis phoned Cowley, who rushed the men from the Marbro to the Biograph, less than a mile away. Cowley was soon on the phone with Hoover who cautioned them to wait outside and not risk a shooting match inside the crowded theater. Each agent was instructed not to endanger himself and was told that if Dillinger offered any resistance, it would be each man for himself.

The Chicago police were not informed of the Dillinger trap. This was largely due to mistrust of some of the local officers who might be sympathetic to the gangster. The theater manager became suspicious of all the agents who were stationed nearby and phoned the precinct. Chicago police responded to what they thought was a robbery. Upon arriving at the Biograph, they were informed by an agent that this was an FBI case, and they did not need the help of the local police. The precinct men departed.

Meanwhile, Cowley arrived on the scene, and Purvis joined him in his car as surveillance continued.

At 10:30 p.m., Dillinger walked out of the theater with his two lady friends. Purvis moved quickly from Cowley's car, joining his men at the theater. He lit his cigar, a prearranged signal that Dillinger had been spotted. Whether Dillinger saw movement in the alley, whether he sensed through his own animal-like instincts that danger threatened, or whether he actually heard the first words of the man behind him that "he is to be taken alive," will never be known. He apparently sensed a trap and drew a pistol from his pocket. As he ran up the alley, a volley of shots rang out as agents zeroed in on the hoodlum. Three shots struck Dillinger, and he fell to the ground, mortally wounded. He was then rushed to Alexian Brothers Hospital where he was pronounced dead at 10:50 p.m. His body was transferred to the county morgue where it was viewed by hundreds of curious people throughout the night. Even though Dillinger had stolen thousands and thousands of dollars, he died with only $7.70 in his pocket.

When Cowley phoned the news to Hoover, the Director shouted "Good job!" Hoover later expressed his commendation in a letter to Cowley: "It was my pleasure last evening to learn of the excellent results, which you attained in the Dillinger hunt. To you as one of those who have actively participated in the planning and direction of this must go a major portion of the credit. Your persistence, patience, and energy have made it possible for us to attain this success, and I am proud and grateful to you.

"You would have been particularly pleased had you been ale to hear the expressions of the Attorney General when I advised him of the results just before he left for his Western trip. He has been so patient and has maintained such confidence in our capacity to make good in this case that I was particularly pleased that it was our agents who finally got this desperado. I want you to know how grateful I am to you, officially and personally, for the help and assistance that you have rendered in this matter, and the manner in which you have directed the same" (Hoover, Letter to Cowley).

As long-standing head of the Chicago field office, Purvis was well-known to the press. This arrangement was fine for Cowley, who had no interest in being in the limelight. So as reporters sought the story on the successful Dillinger manhunt, they consulted Purvis. In press interviews Purvis tended to elevate his own role while downplaying that of Inspector Cowley. Consequently, Purvis was credited as responsible for the manhunt in many of the media accounts. Strands of this revisionist history continue in the movies and television today.

Due to Cowley's outstanding reputation as a respected, responsible person, Hoover made him his official spokesman, directing all news contacts to him.

"I knew the facts concerning Dillinger," Inspector Cowley said, "in all their drab colorlessness and lack of melodrama. I suppose there was not sufficient melodramatic action in Dillinger's last days to satisfy those who thought of him as some kind of legendary buccaneer" (SPC, 191).

"Months from now," Cowley continued, "persons who sheltered or harbored Dillinger who now feel themselves perfectly safe from prosecution will learn that the Bureau has known of their activities all along." Some 27 persons were eventually convicted of harboring, aiding, and abetting Dillinger and his cronies during their reign of terror. With the roundup of these minor players in the Dillinger saga, Cowley and his agents stepped up their activities to rein in the other members of Dillinger's gang. "And the same will be true of every hoodlum who steps up to try to fill his shoes. It is Hoover's intention to make a pariah of every public enemy. It is the sworn duty of every one in the Bureau to help out to their utmost ability to reach that goal" (SPC, 191).

Cowley represented the Bureau at Dillinger's inquest held the day following his death. The hearing record provides a glimpse into Cowley's direct, no-nonsense approach to his work. His testimony demonstrates his ability to follow the course he sets, without waiver. Facing persistent questioning, he pointedly limited his testimony to those matters directly relevant to the inquiry, refusing to be drawn into subjects he deemed not necessary for the public record.

Taking the stand he testified: "The FBI has been conducting an investigation seeking . . . John Dillinger for about a year. Late yesterday afternoon we received the news that Dillinger might attend the Biograph Theater on Lincoln Avenue near Fullerton. We had men stationed there who were able to identify Dillinger when he went in. We had men covering all the exits. We had men to identify him as he left. As he came out, he turned to his left and walked south on Lincoln. Several agents approached him. He drew a gun and was shot and killed" (Dillinger Inquest).

Coroner Frank J. Walsh asked: "Shot by U. S. government agents?"

Cowley replied, "Yes sir."

Deputy Coroner Jacob Schevel asked, "Did he have a gun?"

"Yes sir," Cowley answered, "and he drew it."

Walsh asked, "Was he shot before he could fire?"

Cowley said, "Yes, before he could get his gun into firing position."

Walsh wanted to know, "Who committed this homicide?"

"A government agent," Cowley stated, "properly authorized." Cowley didn't want to name any of the agents, because he felt it would be better for the Bureau if they remained anonymous.

Walsh repeated, "Who committed this homicide?" Cowley gave the same answer: "A government agent, properly authorized."

The agents who fired at Dillinger were in fact Charles B. Winstead, Clarence O. Hurt, and Herman E. Hollis. Each man was commended by Hoover for fearlessness and courageous action. None of them ever said who actually killed Dillinger.

The events of that sultry July evening marked the beginning of the end of the gangster era.

Dillinger's father, John Sr., and half-brother, Hubert, arrived Monday, July 23, to claim the body. Tuesday morning Dillinger's body was transported to Mooresville, Indiana. Once there, the remains were taken to the Harvey Funeral Home where preparations for burial were made. Then the casket was moved to the home of Audrey Hancock, Dillinger's sister, for viewing. The funeral was held there on Wednesday. Dillinger was back home again in Indiana. He was buried at Crown Point Cemetery, Indianapolis.

The three gang molls abandoned at Little Bohemia were arrested by federal agents and whisked off to Madison, Wisconsin, where they were lodged in the county jail awaiting an appearance before Federal Judge Patrick Stone on charges of harboring fugitives from justice.

The girls gave authorities fake names; Marian Marr, Ann Southern, and Rose Ancker. But they refused to give agents any information on the whereabouts of their gangster lovers. They were quartered in the jail under heavy guard, and after several hours of intense grilling by the agents, they began to soften up and give information in exchange for food and rest.

Their true names were Helen Gillis, wife of 'Baby Face' Nelson, Marie Conforti, sweetheart of Homer Van Meter, and Jean Compton, who ran with Tommy Carroll.

All three women were arraigned in Federal Court on May fifth. They all pleaded not guilty and were sentenced to a year and a day at the Federal Prison at Alderson, West Virginia. However, they were later granted probation and released on the condition they would not associate with any criminals (*Wisconsin State Journal*).

All three women ceased to report to their probation officer in Chicago and disappeared shortly after their release. Each woman rejoined her man and continued with him in his life of crime.

9
THE GANGSTER WITH THE BABY FACE

Following Dillinger's death, Nelson became Public Enemy No. 1 and reveled in the glory of being the head gangster in the country. Nelson was characterized by Hoover as the most notorious of the gangsters who plagued the Midwest during the early 1930s.

"I hope the chief will leave me on this assignment until Baby Face Nelson is in the bag," Inspector Cowley told fellow agent Jack DeWitt in the Chicago field office. "Nelson is the most dangerous one of the lot. People put Dillinger on some sort of a pedestal. They did not know him as I did. They know little or nothing about Baby Face. But I know that as long as he is alive, he is a dangerous menace to peace-loving persons wherever he goes. He is a killer—a vicious, crazy killer" (SPC, 194).

No man was better informed of the danger society faced with Nelson at large than was Sam Cowley. However, it was to his chief, Hoover, that Cowley gave the credit for every phase of the removal of 'Pretty Boy' Floyd, every move in tracking down Dillinger, and every bit of detective work tracing the vicious gunman Nelson. "Inspector Cowley never sought publicity," DeWitt explained. "I knew when I talked with him in Chicago that he was the man in whom J. Edgar Hoover had placed great trust and great respect when he assigned him to take the active lead in routing Dillinger from his Chicago hideout" (SPC, 192).

There were traits about Nelson that were studied daily by Cowley before the gunman himself was aware of them. The inspector had already accumulated a swelling file on Nelson.

When Dillinger died, orders from Washington left the dark-eyed, quiet and gentlemanly Cowley still on the trail of Nelson, the nation's worst enemy. A glance at the records showed him that the country held a terrible score against the undersized murderer. A careful study of the records and facts Cowley had compiled informed him of every quirk and phase, every psychological oddity in Nelson's nature. Cowley knew that it was only by possession of such facts that he could hope to capture the wily Nelson.

"There's still a mountain of work to be done," Cowley told DeWitt. "Even when Nelson is accounted for, we'll have to swing into mopping up after a main attack."

"Mr. Hoover has a dynamic personality to begin with," Cowley related. "The men under him know that he is capable, fair and at the same time firm and a believer in strong discipline" (SPC, 193).

"Agents in the (Bureau) working tirelessly towards the end of ridding the county of the Dillingers and the Nelsons were spokes in the wheel of justice," DeWitt observed. "Hoover was the hub. And one of the most important spokes was Samuel P. Cowley."

"I hardly think enough credit has been given the chief. It is he who engineers these things. I am merely a cog in the machinery," Cowley related (SPC, 193).

The Bureau men in every city in America seemed to have the same respect and deep feeling for their chief. This perfect coordination which Hoover had engendered in the department and the respect that every agent and inspector felt for him kept the number of investigators working, not for personal glory, but for the speedy conclusion of the department's work.

Because Cowley believed he might be working in Chicago for a lengthy period, he invited his wife, Lavon, and their two boys to visit him at his apartment. "I made periodic trips to Chicago by train," Lavon said, "taking baby Sam and sometimes taking his three year old brother, John, for a two-week stay." Their two sons were the glory of their lives.

Sam often sent for Lavon and the boys when his out-of-town assignments would allow. And he took every opportunity to visit his extended family when he was assigned to cities where they lived. He carried his love for all of his family throughout his life.

George 'Baby Face' Nelson was born Lester Joseph Gillis, December 6, 1908, in Chicago. His parents were Josef and Mary Gillis, Belgian immigrants who had to struggle to adapt to life in America. Lester grew up in the streets with tough comrades who dubbed him 'Baby Face' due to his juvenile looks. He was also described as "something out of a bad dream." He became one of the toughest and certainly the most heartless of the Depression-era gangsters. FBI files note: "By age 14, Nelson was accomplished at stealing tires, running stills, bootlegging, and armed robbery. In 1922, he was convicted of auto theft and confined to the Chicago Boys' Home. Soon after his release he was caught burglarizing a department store and was returned to the boys' home."

Seeking adventure, Lester threw himself in with underworld kingpin Al Capone as an 'enforcer,' one who used strong-arm tactics to persuade labor leaders to "go along with Capone's operation," so the gangsters could gain control of the labor unions (fbi.org, Lester Gillis).

10

TOO TOUGH FOR BIG AL

At this point, Lester had tasted blood. The switchblade knife, revolver, machine gun, and baseball bat became the tools of his trade. His homicidal temper put him at odds with Capone, a practical man who preferred more peaceful arrangements. So Lester was let go. He soon realized that by lighting out on his own, he could pull in more cash, and wouldn't have to split his ill-gotten gains with the mobsters. Thus, he turned to armed robbery.

He soon met Helen Wawzynak, a salesgirl whom he eventually married.

At 23, Nelson was sent to prison in January, 1931, for a one-year-to-life sentence for a Chicago bank robbery. Following one year's confinement, Nelson was removed from the Illinois State Prison at Joliet to stand trial for another bank robbery in Wheaton, Illinois. He escaped the prison guards while being returned to Joliet and headed west for Reno, Nevada. After a short stay there he fled to Sausalito, California, where he crossed paths with John Paul Chase, a petty bootlegger. They became friends and remained partners in crime for the rest of Nelson's life. Chase was thrilled with the antics Nelson had pulled off, and looked up to him as his gangster hero.

Nelson was soon joined by his wife, Helen, and the couple remained in California until May, 1933. Then they departed for Long Beach, Indiana, where they lived for several months. While in Indiana, Nelson met several criminals, including Homer Van Meter, and occasionally accompanied them on trips to San Antonio, Texas.

Nelson contacted Chase in December, 1933, and asked him to join Nelson in Minneapolis, Minnesota. During a shooting, witnesses reported that the murderers drove a car with California license plates, which were soon traced to Nelson's car. But the trio (Nelson, his wife, Helen, and best friend, Chase) skipped town and ended up in Bremerton, Washington. Helen stayed behind as Nelson and Chase proceeded to Reno, Nevada. Nelson got into an altercation with a man who was a material witness in a U.S. mail fraud case. Nelson killed him during the scuffle.

In April, 1934, Nelson, Helen, and Chase returned to Chicago where they joined up with Dillinger. While Chase remained in the windy city, Nelson and Helen vacationed with the Dillinger gang at Little Bohemia Lodge in Wisconsin.

After escaping from Little Bohemia, Nelson lay low for about a month on an Indian reservation near Lac de Flambeaux, Wisconsin. Slowly and methodically, he worked his way back to Chicago and got lost in the crowd. Helen Gillis had been placed on probation after the Little Bohemia incident. She and Nelson were soon reunited through their underworld connections. They located Chase and the three retreated to a hideout near Lake Geneva, Wisconsin.

Nelson planned to form a new gang, but two of his cohorts, Eddie Green and Tommy Carroll, were dead. The pressure on the Midwestern outlaws was turning the tide of battle, and the FBI was clearly winning the fight. On June 23,

1934, Attorney General Homer Cummings posted a large reward for Nelson's capture.

On June 30, Nelson, Dillinger, and Homer Van Meter robbed the Merchants National Bank of South Bend, Indiana. After the gang fled to Chicago, they laid low in a house on Wolf Road. As two policemen approached the hideout, Nelson opened fire and killed both officers.

After Dillinger's death in July, Nelson, Helen, and Chase decided to head to California until the heat was off. On one occasion, they were stopped for speeding in a small town. After paying a $5 fine at the police station, they were released. If the police had searched Chase's car they would have found it loaded with machine guns, rifles, and ammunition.

In late August, the group returned to Chicago. Within a month, Nelson went to Nevada, and Chase traveled to New York City. Nelson and Chase again joined forces near Minden, Nevada in October, 1934. From there they proceeded to Chicago. On the night of November 26, Nelson, Helen and Chase were cruising just outside the windy city in a Ford pick-up truck Chase had 'obtained' for Nelson some days earlier. Nelson preferred a sedan to the pick-up, so during the early evening hours, Chase and Nelson stole a Ford V-8 sedan belonging to Harold W. Prince of Chicago. Prince reported it missing the following morning.

Later than night, the trio met Clarence Lieder and Joseph Raymond Negri on the Northwest Highway just outside Chicago. The two were freelance robbers, and Negri had worked with Nelson on several crimes early in Nelson's career. Negri, known as 'Fatso,' would use his knowledge of Nelson and other gangsters for sentencing consideration when he was arrested several months later. During the meeting that night Nelson gave Lieder a large sum of money for a sizeable amount of ammunition. They agreed to meet again the following night when Nelson would pick up the purchase.

The morning of Tuesday, November 27, dawned cold and overcast. The weather forecast was for light snow by afternoon.

The trio was staying in a remote cabin in the Lake Geneva, Wisconsin area and rose shortly before noon. Helen prepared a light, cold breakfast and Nelson and Chase made plans to head back to Chicago. They needed to keep the appointment with Lieder and Negri. Nelson was now the most wanted man in America, so he elected to travel by daylight, surmising that it was likely the police would expect him to be on the road only at night. Nelson and Chase made plans to leave within the hour.

Late that afternoon agents confirmed that the trio was briefly at the home of Hobart Hermanson, owner of a resort at Lake Como, Wisconsin.

When Cowley and his agents began the final stages of the hunt for Nelson, they knew that sooner or later he would return to Niles Center, Illinois, as he completed yet another circuit of his hideouts. As the agents watched Niles Center, the search narrowed.

Cowley and his close associate, Special Agent Herman E. Hollis, drew closer to Nelson as every fragment of information from other agents was sifted, examined, and added to the growing pile of clues to the whereabouts of Nelson. Hollis was almost as well-known at FBI headquarters as Cowley, and as trusted by his superiors. Hollis, a native of Des Moines, Iowa, joined the force in 1927 and worked in the Kansas City, Cincinnati and Chicago field offices. For a period of time in 1930, he was acting Special Agent in Charge of the New Orleans field office. He had made a splendid record in Chicago while working under Purvis.

On November 27, Inspector Cowley was alerted to the report of Prince's stolen car. He learned that Nelson had been seen driving a similar automobile in Lake Geneva, Wisconsin. Special Agents James J. Metcalfe and C.B. Winsted spotted Nelson, Helen, and Chase and phoned a warning to Cowley in Chicago. They said the trio was heading toward Chicago on

Route 14, the principal highway connecting northeast Illinois to Wisconsin. Cowley dispatched Special Agents William Ryan and Thomas McDade to search the area for Nelson.

They met up with Nelson near Fox River Grove, Illinois, northwest of Chicago. He was accompanied by Helen and Chase. McDade was driving, and he swung his car around and began following the trio. Nelson spied the agents, in spite of their attempt to keep a low profile by driving an old borrowed 1928 Ford. Nelson quickly made a U-turn and headed back north. Within seconds the two vehicles passed again. Before Ryan and McDade could react, Nelson made another U-turn and began gaining on the agents' car.

"I'm going to try to stay ahead of them," McDade told Ryan. "Hold your speed and let Nelson catch up with us," Ryan replied. As they passed through Fox River Grove, McDade kept an eye on Nelson in his rear view mirror as Nelson's Ford grew closer. Nelson suddenly shot forward and drew along side the agents. "Pull over," Nelson shouted. "Pull over!" Nelson was firing a pistol at the agents with his right hand while he tried to steer the car with his left. Being left handed, he attempted to switch the pistol to his left hand and put his right hand on the wheel, and nearly lost control of the car. As Nelson fell back a few feet, Chase, in the back seat, began firing his automatic rifle at the agents through his own window. The agents were armed only with their pistols, but Ryan opened fire at Nelson's car through his rear window. As the agents drove through Barrington, McDade noticed Nelson was no longer visible in his rear view mirror. McDade kept driving on to Palatine where he stopped to let Nelson catch up with him.

11
COWLEY VS. NELSON

Meanwhile, Cowley and Hollis were on their way to back up Ryan and Metcalf. They encountered the running gun battle headed in a northerly direction between Barrington and Fox River Grove. Cowley promptly turned his Hudson around and joined the chase. As they approached Barrington, Nelson spotted Cowley and Hollis approaching from the rear in their automobile. At the same time, Nelson's car began to sputter. Ryan's bullets had struck the radiator and fuel pump. This was later confirmed by Joe Duncan, a truck driver who told police that when Nelson's car passed him on Highway 14 it was leaking fluid heavily. With his car disabled and the second FBI vehicle nearly at his bumper, Nelson had little choice but to pull off the road into a field in Barrington.

Nelson and Chase rolled from their stricken auto, Nelson brandishing a submachine gun and Chase clutching his automatic rifle. Nelson dragged Helen into a shallow roadside ditch, warning her to keep her head down. Agents Cowley and Hollis took up defensive positions, ready to shoot, but held their fire until they were dead sure of their targets. ("Special agents take extraordinary precautions to avoid the possibility of wounding innocent citizens," Hoover had said.) (*Saga*).

Chase crouched behind the disabled car, rested his rifle on the hood, and stared in disbelief as Nelson walked openly between the vehicles, machine gun in hand. Then both criminals blasted away at the agents. The noise was ear-splitting as crossfire erupted. Hollis was killed outright with a single bullet to the head from Chase's rifle. Nelson shuffled forward, squeezing the trigger. Nelson slowly moved toward Cowley. Cowley's bullets tore Nelson's legs, torso, chest, and shoulder, shredding his clothes to rags.

Sam didn't falter. More bullets struck Nelson but still he moved forward toward Cowley. Though mortally wounded from a single rifle bullet to the abdomen, Cowley kept firing at Nelson, but he kept coming. Cowley emptied his machine gun into the advancing outlaw. Finally, Nelson slumped to the ground, too weak to carry on.

Cowley, bleeding profusely from his abdominal wound, was barely alive. Nelson's machine-gunfire had been wild, as he obviously missed hitting either agent. Chase had shot both of them.

Chase, who had escaped injury during the incident, ran to Nelson and dragged him into Cowley's car. Then he moved ammunition from Nelson's embattled auto to Cowley's Hudson. "Where's Helen?" Chase asked. "I don't know," Nelson replied. "Let's get out of here." For the second time, Nelson was willing to abandon Helen. But she ran to the car, climbed in, and the trio sped away.

The gun battle lasted less than five minutes. In a statement given by Lavon Cowley, she reported that she had received a letter from a young man in a nearby service station who had witnessed the battle. As he approached the fallen agents, he realized Agent Hollis had been killed. Inspector Cowley asked him to notify the Chicago FBI office (Lavon). A nearby road maintenance crew who also witnessed the gunfight said Nelson looked like a gangster in the movies as he walked toward the agents firing his machine gun from his hip.

State Trooper William Gallagher stopped his cruiser near the site where the gun battle was raging. He took refuge in a nearby service station. When the battle ended, Trooper Gallagher ran to Sam's rescue. As he lay near death, Sam struggled to tell the officer: "We are Federal men. Take care of my partner (Hollis) first" (SPC, 6).

As Agents Ryan and McDade raced back to the scene, they found Hollis dead and Cowley barely clinging to life. "Did they get Hollis?" Sam asked. "If so, help him. Forget me." Sam was unaware that Hollis had died. A passing motorist had stopped to render help. He was asked to drive Sam to the nearest hospital while Ryan and McDade headed out to pick up Nelson's trail.

Cowley was rushed to Sherman Hospital in Elgin, Illinois, by W. G. Rossman, a car salesman who was driving by. Lavon was soon at Sam's side. He greeted her lovingly, then asked to talk to Purvis who was also in the room. It was in this hushed conversation that Cowley related to Purvis the details of how Chase had shot him and Hollis.

After inquiring about his partner's condition, Cowley lapsed into a coma that lasted for the next six hours. At 2:20 the next morning, Cowley, in deep shock from hemorrhaging, quietly slipped away. He had at last completed his assignment to bring down the evil gangsters (Lavon).

Inspector Cowley had acted under the personal direction of J. Edgar Hoover to smash the worst ring of predatory criminals this nation has ever known and to upset the politico-criminal ring that terrorized the Midwest for so long. The same relentless spirit and stark heroism that sent his Mormon ancestors across the plains to hew out a place of living in the mountain west drove Sam Cowley to his grave.

Assistant FBI Director Harold Nathan said of Cowley: "As generations of new agents come into our service they will be told of . . . Sam Cowley. He will become a tradition. He will have attained earthly immortality. Fate . . . forced him to play a part for which I believe he had little taste, but which he played out to the end.

"Sam went down, but his gun was blazing and he was shooting straight. It was his bullets that killed (Baby Face) Nelson. . . . This is the price that civilization has always demanded of its defenders. Civilization is built upon the blood of its martyrs and the tears of its widows and orphans" (SPC, 21-24).

FBI Director J. Edgar Hoover said, "When I said Sam Cowley was the bravest man I have ever known it is not because he shot it out with 'Baby Face' Nelson nor yet because he directed the manhunt which trapped and finished that other public enemy John Dillinger. Many another special agent of the FBI would have acted precisely as Sam did in similar circumstances. Some people don't realize that when a special agent of the FBI faces a gangster and known killer, the agent is not just another man with a badge and a gun. He is a man with a badge, a gun, and a mission in which he believes. That mission is to prove to any who may doubt, they of high or low degree, that in these United States truth has substance and justice will not be denied. If the accomplishment of that mission requires that he surrender his life, the agent will do so, just as Sam did and as scores of special agents have done before and since. Sam Cowley's courage was beyond heroics."

"He was brave enough to be scrupulously honest in little things as well as big things. He didn't accept the easy way out, a half-truth, a white lie, or a turned head. It is said of Sam by those who knew him best that he never told a lie in his life. I know for a fact that he knew what was right and did what was right, regardless of provocation. That's the kind of courage that can carry a man proudly form the cradle to the grave. Sam had no false pride. There wasn't a pretentious bone in his body. He was honestly ambitious.

"From the beginning Sam was a man who lived his work. He served his investigative apprenticeship in various Division offices where his abilities became so manifest that he was called in to the Seat of Government at Washington, DC to fill an executive position.

"One wonders what makes such a man as Sam. I think one of my co-workers found the answer. This man said that Sam never spoke to him about matters of religion, but that his attitude and bearing were those of a man whose faith was rooted in certain basic certainties and who knew that results were beyond human responsibility and power. His was the calm of a man who did his best and left the final decision to a Higher Power. Sam was deeply and devoutly religious, a man of great faith. The longer I live the more certain I become that faith is the source of strength which enables men to hold to their duty in the face of overwhelming odds. I am just as certain that faith is the sustaining fact which holds men to the monotonous but necessary tasks which go into making up so much of living. Good law enforcement requires men of faith" (Hoover, Marriott Letter).

12

THE AFTERMATH

At the time her son was mortally wounded in the fight with Nelson, Luella P. Cowley was attending a Relief Society meeting in the 17th Ward in Salt Lake City. She began to feel strangely worried and said to a friend, "I feel that something is happening to someone close to me. I don't know what it is, but I am frightened. I feel like someone in my family is dying."

Mrs. Cowley was not usually a nervous woman, but she finally grew so concerned that she left the meeting, saying that she knew something was wrong. When she returned home, a neighbor phoned to tell the family that she had heard the news from Chicago on the radio (*Deseret News Magazine*, 5).

Rossman, the Good Samaritan car salesman who had stopped to help the fallen agents, was so moved by his experience getting Sam to the hospital that he wrote Lavon: "Mr. Cowley . . . proved to me that an ideal, self-sacrificing American really did exist, and this fact has been on my mind ever since I helped (Sam) into (my) automobile that fatal day" (Rossman).

Chase and Helen drove the wounded Nelson to Father Philip W. Coughlan, then to a hideout in Winnetka, Illinois, where he died around eight o'clock that evening.

The next day, agents found his nude body wrapped in a blanket, lying in a cemetery near Niles Center. His body had sustained 17 bullet wounds. Ballistics tests later showed that .45-caliber bullets from Cowley's gun killed Nelson. He was later buried in St. Joseph's Cemetery, River Grove, Illinois.

Nelson's sister, Juliet Fitzsimmons, remarked that he was a "clever kid, and the only way they could ever bring him in was on a slab."

A few days after Nelson's death, Helen Gillis gave herself up to police and was returned to Madison, Wisconsin, for probation violations, along with Marie Conforti and Jean Crompton. As they appeared again before Judge Stone, he revoked their probation and ordered them to finish out their sentences at Alderson, West Virginia.

Helen told the judge that she violated her probation because "I knew (Nelson) didn't have long to live, and I wanted to be with him as long as I could" (*Wisconsin State Journal*).

Sam had been a capable leader to hundreds of FBI agents, inspired to do what was right no matter what the cost. In the end, he laid down his life that others might be spared the evil effects of the horrible gangsters who pillaged and killed during those Depression years. There was no finer tribute than his father's: "Sam was one of God's noblemen."

Sam's body lay in state at the Utah Capitol Building in Salt Lake City, so his many family members and friends could pay homage to him. Family, Church, and civic leaders gathered at the Assembly Hall on Temple Square for a memorial service (SPC 1-50). The eulogy and remarks leave no doubt about Sam's character and his reputation in law enforcement. For J. Edgar Hoover, the loss was profound; he'd lost a personal friend as well as a brave agent. The most heart-warming remarks came in the opening prayer, offered by Sam's brother, Matthew, and in the eulogy, given by Sam's father, Mathias.

In delivering the invocation, Sam's brother Matthew Cowley characterized him as a man of "fine qualities and characteristics." In prayer he honored their parents: "That through them we have received normal intellects and sound bodies. We are proud to bear their name, and in behalf of my brother, I thank Thee for those parents, which bore him and which reared him in the house of righteousness, that every actuating impulse of his life was one of goodness and not of evil . . .

"At this time we ask Thy blessings upon his fellows with whom he labored in the great national service, for the defense of life, liberty and property; that through the spilling of his blood they may be spared a similar untimely end" (See Appendix for entire text).

Sam's brother-in-law, President Edgar B. Brossard of the Washington, DC Branch of the Church said, "Samuel used his own mind and made his own decisions. He was a man of firm convictions and fearless in maintaining them . . . . Sam was devoted to his wife and children. The love and inspiration of them were always with him. He was full of pride and pleasure and future anticipation for them. Sam had a profound testimony of the gospel of Jesus Christ. Sam was genuinely happy and enthusiastic in his work with the (FBI). He showed special ability in this investigational type of work and maintained a drive within him characteristic of true missionary zeal.

"If all citizens were as valiant in their support of the government of this great land [as Sam Cowley], we would have no need for sacrificing men on such missions."

Elder Harold W. Langton of the bishopric of the 17th Ward, the home ward of Sam's parents, said, "This splendid man gave his life in the protection of our interests and is entitled to all the honor that we can give him."

"A young man gave his all that American ideals might be preserved," said Gus P. Backman, secretary of the Salt Lake City Chamber of Commerce. "Sam Cowley contributed his life in an effort to uphold and defend the Constitution. He died in safeguarding for posterity the principles of justice, freedom and democracy.... His deeds alone can praise him.... Sam was inspired with courage by God Almighty, and we pray that He will look with tender kindness upon the widow and the family, that He will bestow the same courage upon them in facing this loss that guided Sam in his efforts in behalf of his country."

John M. Knight, Salt Lake City commissioner of public safety, said, "We have only words of praise and commendation for (Sam's) courage, fidelity, and devotion to duty. It mattered not with Inspector Cowley whether he was on the farm or at school or in the mission field, or serving as a lawyer or a Department of Justice agent, he lived his work, undaunted and unafraid. His progenitors were among those who braved the trials of frontier life and played an important role in the development of this great commonwealth. Sam pursued his course diligently and relentlessly until he had completed his task, even to the laying down of his life for his friends. It was the Master who said: Greater love hath no man than this, that a man will lay down his life for his friend."

Apostle John A. Widtsoe remarked of Sam, "His whole life is but the reflection of the teachings of his home, the philosophy that he was there taught, and which he accepted and used in his daily life... I trust and pray that the type of home that made Sam Cowley may continue to flourish among us, for the safety of our republic, and the safety of the institution of our fathers who laid the foundations of this country, for it will depend on that type of home for that type of training that guided the officer whose body lies before us today....

"I want to say to those who have been bereaved that we have the divine promise which will never fail. The Father of us all has promised that He will remember the widow and the fatherless. I can tell you from my own experience that the Lord does remember the widow and the fatherless, and let this older sister who has been such a splendid companion to her husband rest upon this divine promise that all will be well with her."

Agent Henry C. Taggart, of the U.S. Secret Service, said, "I knew him as a good clean living, honest man and a fearless officer. What more could be said of anyone? I congratulate his wife and the family of this good man, that the Lord has been good to them, that He has instilled in their hearts such a faith that they know for a certainty that they will meet their loved one again."

Utah Governor Henry H. Blood: "The State of Utah has given one of her brilliant and courageous sons to the cause of major crime control . . . . But his death will not have been in vain. There will be . . . renewed determination to stamp out crime and checkmate vicious criminals. Our country must be purged of lawlessness . . . . Samuel P. Cowley, the State you have so highly honored pays tribute to your faithfulness and your great worth as a citizen and an officer."

Apostle George Albert Smith said that Sam Cowley was "trained in a home that believed in God, trained in a community that believed in God, living in a day when the power of our Heavenly Father is so necessary to meet our problems, he went out to bring honor and credit to the name he bore, to bring satisfaction to his friends and loved ones . . . . I have wondered if we really appreciate, in our homes, what it means to live in an organized government, and to have as our friends those who for a small pittance jeopardize their lives day by day, in order that we may have the comforts and blessings that we enjoy . . . . If the people of this world would only conform their lives to the teachings that the Redeemer of mankind gave to us, and to the teachings of the prophets of God who have lived upon this earth, happiness would be in every home; joy and satisfaction would abide in every heart; and the thing we call death would not have the sting that it does now, because we would all know that it is but stepping from mortal life into a more perfect existence, where we may all live if we will keep the commandments of our Heavenly Father. . . ."

Sam's sister Laura said, "Sam died just as he lived—courageous and determined to do what was right." Lavon Cowley said, "He did give his life in the call of duty and for mankind."

Probably the finest tribute came from Sam's father, Matthias. "Sam was honest in every sense of the word. He was courageous and knew no fear. He is moral, temperate and industrious, possessing a character without a blemish. He was indeed one of God's noblemen" (See Appendix for entire text).

The following communications were read at the service:

U.S. Attorney General Homer Cummings wired his condolences to Lavon Cowley: "I am deeply grieved by the death of your husband. I know him personally as a man of fine character, and as a capable and fearless officer."

J. Edgar Hoover, FBI Director, wrote to Mrs. Cowley: "Sam's death is an irreparable loss to our Division. His tireless energy and high personal standards won the confidence of all who came into relationship with him. An unvarying courtesy, which never sacrificed principle for the sake of advantage, won him the respect and confidence of his circle of friends. Not only officially have I lost one of the ablest and most indefatigable workers, but personally, I have lost a dear and loyal friend, and his place can never be taken, either in our affections or in his official work...."

In the days following the memorial service, the following citations were issued:

Director Hoover honored Sam posthumously: "There was further promotion in store for him, and I had intended to rely more and more upon his proven ability.... Inspector Cowley deserves the credit for many of our important arrests.... Sam Cowley, in charge of the Special Squad, deserves the credit for perfecting the arrangements that resulted in the location and killing of John Dillinger. Sam's command was supreme in the Chicago region; all members of the Chicago office were cognizant of his overall plan. It was he who mapped the campaign, working from a secret office with unlisted telephones, and it was this campaign which led to Dillinger's death.... It was due to Sam's modesty that the general public did not know the true facts concerning the downfall of our most publicized ruffian of recent years ... 'I'd just rather stay in the dark as I've been doing,' Sam had told me over the telephone. 'Besides, I've got some good information on 'Baby Face' Nelson, and I'll just stay under cover here in Chicago and work it out.'

"Sam Cowley had true courage," Hoover remarked. "I have said many times that Sam was the bravest man I ever knew. That belief is based on something more than the knowledge that he had the physical and mental fortitude to go out and face kill-crazy gangsters whose false courage lasted only while they had lead in their guns. "Sam was a plain, direct, devout man with the simplicity of true worth, honor and dignity. His whole life was based on simple faith and determination to do his duty."

The Theta Beta Chapter Sigma Chi Fraternity award went to Cowley posthumously in 1935, accepted by his brother Joseph F. Cowley.

The Utah State University Alumni Association honored Sam: "Samuel P. Cowley has made a great record; and he died while performing an imperative social duty. His service was magnificent; his loss tragic. We are proud of the fact that he attended this institution for many years, and we shall be happy if just a few of our students perform anything like (his) comparable service to their country ...."

Fastened to the wall in the entrance to Old Main on the campus of Utah State University in Logan is a simple bronze plaque reading:

> IN MEMORY OF SAMUEL PARKINSON COWLEY CLASS OF 1925 WHO DIED IN THE SERVICE OF HIS COUNTRY NOVEMBER 28 1934 FOR THE CAUSE OF JUSTICE AND THE SAFETY OF HIS FELLOW MEN

Sam, his valiant partner, Herman Hollis, and their fellow agent Carter Baum joined with three other agents in the Hall of Honor, for FBI agents killed as the direct result of an adversarial action. Special Agent Edwin C. Shanahan was killed in 1925, Special Agent Paul E. Reynolds died in 1929, and Special Agent Raymond J. Caffrey was slain during the Kansas City Massacre in 1933.

13
THE TRIAL

John Paul Chase, whom Hoover tagged a 'nobody in the annals of crime,' was indicted in Chicago for murdering both Inspector Sam Cowley and Special Agent Herman Hollis.

Chase was born December 26, 1901 in California where he spent most of his life.

He attended school through the fifth grade, then worked as a ranch hand near San Rafael. He later worked in railway shops for four years, first as an office boy, then as a machinist's apprentice. In 1930 he became associated with a liquor smuggling operation comprised of persons with strong underworld connections.

At the time Nelson arrived in California, Chase was involved with a bootlegging gang. Nelson and Chase worked as armed guards for the truck used to illegally transport liquor.

As the two became close friends, Chase began introducing Nelson as his half-brother.

Writing in *Persons In Hiding*, Hoover said, "The public never had heard of Chase. So unknown was he that after Nelson's death (and after disposing of Cowley's Hudson car), he walked without danger into a police station, where he was photographed for a chauffeur's license, by which action he obtained a job as the convoy driver of a fleet of motor cars from the factory to the Pacific Coast.

"He had no fingerprint record, nor even a previous arrest. Yet in his short, tragic career lies one of the most dramatic stories behind the big guns of crime . . . . Chase picked the wrong man to emulate. Another person in his position might have wanted to be a famous engineer, or an aviator, or a motion picture actor. Chase chose to follow a bandit, and thus became an outstanding example . . . of youth at a crossroads, (who) has walked down the wrong road into the jungles of crime" (Hoover, *Persons*, 100).

In early December, 1934, special agents of the FBI's San Francisco Office contacted Chase's former employers and associates. They were instructed to notify the FBI if Chase was seen. On December 27, Chase tried to borrow money from employees at a Mount Shasta, California fish hatchery, where he had worked in 1928. The FBI and local police were immediately notified and Police Chief A. L. Roberts apprehended Chase without incident.

Chase was returned to Chicago December 31. On February 19, 1935, he was arraigned before Judge Phillip L. Sullivan in the U.S. District Court in Chicago. Chase pleaded not guilty to two counts of murder in the deaths of Hollis and Cowley.

The Associated Press reported the following trial account: The trial for Cowley's murder began March 18. Chase was the first person to be tried under a new law that made it a Federal offense to kill an agent while in the performance of his duties. The law required that the trial must be held in Federal court, and a guilty verdict mandated the death sentence unless the jury recommended life imprisonment. The case was prosecuted by U. S. Attorney Dwight H. Green.

Special Agent James J. Metcalf was the first witness for the prosecution. He testified that Chase was with 'Baby Face'

Nelson and his wife, Helen Gillis, on November 27, 1934, when he and his partner, Special Agent A. E. Winstead spotted them at Lake Geneva, Wisconsin.

To support an argument that the criminals did not start the gunfight, defense counsel W. W. O'Brien claimed that the bullet holes in Nelson's windshield had come from the Agents' guns, but FBI technicians testified that the nature of the bullet holes showed that they were fired from inside the car.

Prosecutor Green stated that the angle of the path of the bullet which struck Cowley "proved that it was fired by Chase." The prosecution indicated they would rely on Cowley's death bed statement to Special Agent Melvin Purvis that Chase had shot him and killed Hollis.

O'Brien indicated that he would contend that Cowley was incoherent and unconscious when Purvis was in Cowley's hospital room and could not have made such a statement.

However, Dr. Morgan Carpenter, who had performed surgery on Cowley at the hospital, testified that "Cowley was perfectly conscious during the first hours of his hospitalization. He joked with the nurses, telling them to inform his wife that he would be late for dinner. When Mrs. Cowley reached his bedside, he recognized her and said 'Hello, Sweetheart.'"

The Reverend Philip Coughlan, a priest, related how Helen and Chase brought the wounded Nelson to him in Wilmette, Illinois, shortly after the gun battle. Father Coughlan testified how he started to lead them to a hospital to get medical help for Nelson, but they dropped from behind his car and disappeared.

The jury found Chase guilty of murdering Cowley, and they made a recommendation of life in prison. "Apparently the jury didn't believe Chase and Nelson were the aggressors," O'Brien remarked, "or they wouldn't have recommended a life sentence."

But Hoover's ongoing orders that the gangsters were to be taken alive if possible, casts doubt that Hollis and Cowley had been the aggressors.

Mrs. Herman Hollis, widow of Agent Hollis, sat through the trial with her one-year-old child. She later told Prosecutor Green, "I'm glad he's put away." Lavon Cowley, seeking to avoid any appearance of vengeance, did not attend the proceedings. At last there was closure for the Hollis and Cowley families.

At the direction of the U.S. Attorney General, Chase was to serve his life term at Alcatraz, the nation's highest security prison. Chase began his incarceration there March 31. Inmates housed at Alcatraz were not eligible for parole. But if and when they were transferred to a lower security facility, parole would be possible. Chase served his time there until September, 1954, when he was transferred to Leavenworth.

Chase had then hoped for a parole, but was still under indictment for the murder of Agent Hollis. Chase's attorney filed a motion in Chicago Federal Court in 1955 requesting an immediate trial or a dismissal. On October 17, a U.S. District Judge dismissed the indictment, ruling that Chase's knowledge of the indictment and his failure to take action did not constitute a waiver of his right to a speedy trial.

After repeated attempts, Chase was finally paroled in October, 1966, and died of cancer in California in October, 1973.

EPILOGUE

Lavon held up well under the strain and raised her two boys, John and Sam Jr., in the love and grace that she was known for. "I had many wonderful experiences in my five years with Sam," Lavon Cowley said. "I didn't think his work was more dangerous than many others. Accidents happen to every category of people. I felt it was his time to die. My saddest thoughts were that his sons could not know their father, and that he couldn't watch them grow up.

"After Sam's death, Mr. Hoover told me I could go to work for the FBI. When Sam Jr. was two, we went to the Los Angeles FBI office in 1936. I was chief clerk there. I had to go back to work, because we had no other source of income after Sam died. I worked for the Bureau for 11 years in the Los Angeles, Washington, DC, and Salt Lake City offices" (Lavon).

Helen Gillis finished out her term at the women's federal prison at Alderson, West Virginia. She never took her maiden name back. Helen died in 1987 at age 79. And true to her gangster husband to the end, she was laid to rest beside Nelson in the River Grove cemetery with a simple tomb stone reading: "WIFE, HELEN GILLIS."

Purvis retired from the Bureau in July, 1935, after a falling out with Hoover. Failure of the FBI to effectively halt Anna Sage's deportation further soured Purvis. He did a promotion for a breakfast cereal firm where he enlisted youngsters to join his Junior G-Man Club. By sending in a dime and a box top from Post Toasties, a young man could get a tin badge and a document certifying that he was indeed one of Purvis' Junior G-Men. Purvis died at his own hand February 29, 1960, in South Carolina.

Anna Sage continued her struggle to remain in this country. She had been paid $5,000, her share of the reward money, for fingering Dillinger. Cowley delivered it personally to her. In spite of the recommendations from Cowley and Purvis, the government proceeded with deportation proceedings. On October 16, 1934, her case was heard in Federal District Court in Chicago. The court ruled against her. She appealed to the U.S. Court of Appeals who upheld the lower court decision. In April, 1936, Anna Sage, aka Ana Cumpanas, was returned to her native Rumania where she died in April, 1947.

After serving the longest term of any inmate in Alcatraz—25 years and one month—Alvin Karpis was paroled in 1969 and deported to his native Canada. Four years later he relocated to Spain where he died while playing golf in 1973. He was 79.

J. Edgar Hoover continued as director of the FBI, serving under five more presidents until his death in 1972.

Federal Prosecutor Dwight H. Green went on to serve as Illinois governor from 1941 to 1949.

Doc Moran ran a string of hideouts along with his position as medic to the mobs, and he became quite wealthy from fees he received for concealing crooks and percentage takes for helping launder stolen funds. As greed will do, it affected Doc to the point of quarreling with his felonious friends, and they became suspicious of him. As he was given to heavy drinking and loose blabbering, his underworld cronies began to fear him to the extent that they dropped him into Lake Erie chained to a railroad iron. His body was never recovered.

Today a bronze plaque marks the spot where Sam Cowley and Herman Hollis fell in Barrington, Illinois, on that fateful day in November, 1934. Mounted on a red granite rock beside a flagpole flying the stars and strips, in the shade of a locust tree, the monument reads:

In Memory of Special Agent W. Carter Baum, Special Agent Herman E. Hollis, and Inspector Samuel P. Cowley: FBI Chicago Field Office. "You cannot choose your battlefield. The gods do that for you, but you can plant a standard where a standard never flew."
—Nathalia Crane

In the early 1930s our nation experienced a dramatic rise in violent crime and criminal activity. John Dillinger and Lester Gillis, a.k.a. Baby Face Nelson, were two of the more notorious Midwest outlaws of this era. The men and women of the Chicago Field Office of the FBI played an important role in combatting this crime problem, and three employees made the ultimate sacrifice.

On April 22, 1934, FBI Special Agents W. Carter Baum and J. C. Newman both from The Chicago FBI office along with a local constable, raided a hideout of Baby Face Nelson at Koerner's Corners, Wisconsin. In an ensuing gun battle Special Agent Baum was killed. Special Agent Newman and the constable were wounded. Nelson escaped.

At this site on November 27, 1934, FBI Inspector Samuel P. Cowley and Special Agent Herman E. Hollis, both of the Chicago office, attempted to apprehend then Public Enemy No. 1, Baby Face Nelson. A running gun battle ensued along Illinois Highway 14, which ended near the entrance to Langendorf Park. Both Hollis and Cowley were mortally wounded, as was Nelson.

This plaque is dedicated in grateful memory to these FBI employees who gave their lives in the performance of their sworn duties.

Presented by: Current and Former FBI employees, Chicago Field Office Society of Former Special Agents of the FBI, Chicago Chapter FBI National Academy Associates, Illinois Chapter.

APPENDIX

Excerpts from the Samuel P. Cowley memorial services, Assembly Hall, Temple Square, Salt Lake City, Utah (SPC, 1-50).

Invocation, Elder Matthew Cowley, brother of Samuel P. Cowley
(SPC, 1-2)

Oh God, our Holy Father, we come before Thee this day in a house of mourning, and acknowledge Thee as the giver of all life and the giver of all blessings to human life. Father, it is Thy power to give and Thy power to take away, and we are pleased to bless Thy name for this power which Thou hast made manifest in perpetuating the life into eternity of our son, husband and brother.

We thank Thee for the blessings that come through visiting the house of mourning, that we are brought nearer to Thee, and that we participate in the achievements of one who has lived nobly and died nobly. Father, forbid that those who belonged to him, those of us who remain, shall ever utter the language of complaint.

"Let it be enough for our faith, that the whole creation groans with mortal frailty; but strive with unconquerable constancy, and surely not all in vain."

Our Father, we thank Thee this day for our parentage, that through them we have received normal intellects and sound bodies. We are proud to bear their name, and in behalf of my brother I thank Thee for those parents which bore him and which reared him in the house of righteousness, that every actuating impulse of his life was one of goodness and not of evil. May we live to honor his name by righteous effort. May we honor him with deeds, by reflecting his fine qualities and characteristics.

Father, at this time we ask Thy blessings upon his fellows with whom he labored in the great national service, for the defense of life, liberty and property; that through the spilling of his blood they may be spared a similar untimely end.

We ask Thee to bless his parents, that they may have a feeling of reconciliation for all that has been done, that they may know, as they have always known, and as they have taught him to know, that mortality is but a flash in the pan of immortality; that we pass from this mortal coil into an eternal life which affords greater opportunity for service, closer contact with Thee and with Thy Son, Jesus Christ.

Bless his wife, his helpmeet, who has been with him but a brief span of years, that the memory of that companionship may sustain her in the hours of loneliness. They have borne two beautiful children to perpetuate his name. Father, may Thy spirit radiate the environs of her home, or wherever she may be; that from now on Thy spirit may be her guide and companion to assist her in the rearing of her children, their children, that in Thine own due time these children may live to serve as he has served, and bear his name in honor before Thee.

Bless all of us who mourn, that from this moment we may pledge a renewed devotion to the simple philosophy of Thy son, Jesus Christ, which we believe sincerely to be the only power under Heaven, which will regenerate us and save us and exalt us in Thy celestial kingdom and presence.

Bless all those who are attached to this our departed brother, as son, husband and father. Bless them that they may reflect the ideals for which he died; that our homes, our state and our nation, may be better places in which to live.

God bless these services. Be with us throughout this day, and until it shall be our privilege and blessing to meet him again face to face, and have him say to us, as we say to him: "Well done. Enter into thy rest and thy glory."

These blessings and favors we ask, ascribing unto Thee all the honor, the praise and the glory, in the name of Thy Son, Jesus Christ, Amen.

Eulogy by Matthias F. Cowley, Sam s father
(SPC, 46-50)

Samuel Parkinson Cowley was born of goodly lineage, as was Nephi of old. On his father's side he was the descendant of men who fought in the Revolutionary War for the freedom of the American Colonies. On his mother's side he was a descendant of the noblest sons and daughters of England. On both paternal and maternal lines his progenitors were men and women all along the line down to his generation, who were moral, temperate, and industrious, always numbered with the good citizens of the communities and countries in which they dwelt.

The gospel restored to earth through the Prophet Joseph Smith found his ancestors ready to receive it. His great-grandparents on both sides of the house embraced this gospel and their generations following down to this time have been faithful adherents to The Church of Jesus Christ of Latter-day Saints, and of such was the earthly origin of Samuel P. Cowley.

Samuel Parkinson Cowley was born July 23, 1899, in Franklin, Idaho, the son of Matthias Foss Cowley and Luella Parkinson Cowley. He was the fifth son in a family of nine sons and six daughters. He was honored with his birth in the oldest town in Idaho and one of the first of the Latter-day Saint colonies north of the line dividing Utah from Idaho. The town of Franklin was equally honored by having Samuel for one of her noblest sons, and many noble men and women began their mortal life in that little village.

While Samuel was six years old the family moved to Preston, Idaho, the headquarters of the Oneida Stake of Zion. While there he attended the District School and reached the fifth grade. At the age of 11 years, with his mother and three other children, he moved to Logan City, Utah, where he further pursued his studies at the Benson, Whittier and Lowell grade schools and the Logan High School.

At the age of eight, the age as appointed by revelation for children to be baptized, he was baptized on his birthday anniversary, July 23, 1907, by his father, Matthias F. Cowley, and confirmed by his grandfather, Samuel Rose Parkinson. In line with his initiation into the Church, he was baptized in the Logan Temple for 150 souls, who had died without the gospel.

He was ordained a deacon when 12 years of age, October 23, 1911, by John Q. Adams, bishop of the Fifth Ward in the Cache Valley Stake of Zion. Samuel was ordained a teacher by Elder Charles W. Batt, bishop's counselor in the Fifth Ward of Logan, when he was 15 years of age, October 21, 1915. He was faithful in the discharge of his duties in both the deacons and teachers quorums and became a counselor in the presidency of both quorums.

He was ordained an elder on January 17, 1917, by Bishop John Q. Adams and the same month in obedience to the divine call, he was set apart and left home to fill a mission in the Hawaiian Islands. He was absent on this mission three years and nine months. He readily acquired the Hawaiian language and spoke with freedom to the understanding of the natives. He baptized a few and was instrumental in blessing children, and in administering to those who were sick and afflicted. He assisted by manual labor to build a chapel in Laie and in getting up bazaars to raise money to erect the temple of the Lord in Hawaii, besides contributing of his own money used for his support in the mission field.

Before leaving for his mission, while living in Logan, and when only 13 years of age he procured employment during the summer vacation, cutting lawns and doing other work for the Agricultural College. This was the first salaried job he ever had. With the first earned money and when sufficient, he bought a nice down quilt and presented it to his mother for a Christmas present. We have enjoyed the use of the quilt ever since, and it seems that much dearer now that Samuel has passed away.

Before his release from the Hawaiian mission he made a visit to all the islands in the group. In visiting the Leper Island, the home of those afflicted with the terrible disease of leprosy, he was deeply impressed with the patience and cheerfulness of the lepers as they sang and played the ukulele. It was a lesson to Samuel of the patience, and fortitude of the afflicted colony. He thought them an example worthy to be followed by all other people.

He reached his home in Logan in the fall of 1921 and entered the Utah Agricultural College as a student. He majored in economics. While attending the college, he earned some money by working for the institution. He went to Nebraska, North and South Dakota during the summer vacations from school selling knit goods for the Union Knitting Mills of Logan, Utah. At the end of his first day at selling, which was in North Platte, Nebraska, his sister Laura—also selling there with her husband—asked him how he had gotten along. He replied that he hadn't sold much but had held "some wonderful gospel conversations." The spirit of his mission continued with him, and asserted itself whenever opportunity occurred to let people know that he was a Latter-day Saint and to explain the gospel to them. This same good spirit we are thankful to say remained with him to the end of mortal life.

In 1923 he graduated with honor from the Agricultural College. Soon after graduation he went to Washington, DC, having in view the study and practice of law. He had no funds with which to enter the law school, but after considerable time and effort he secured employment in Woodward and Lathrup's department store.

Shortly thereafter he enrolled as a law student in the George Washington University. He was quick to learn and also he was a hard worker—never a quitter—and what he learned, he remembered, and made application in a practical way of the knowledge thus acquired. His key to continued effort was the work of the scripture, "The race is not to the swift nor the battle to the strong."

While attending law school in Washington he served as secretary to Dr. Edgar B. Brossard, a member of the U.S. Tariff Commission. He passed the District of Columbia Bar Examination in December, 1928, and received his graduation diploma from the George Washington University Law School in the spring of 1929.

Upon completion of his academic training he received an appointment as Special Agent for the Federal Bureau of Investigation, U.S. Department of Justice. After the initial training period in Washington he was first stationed in Los Angeles, where he served for nearly one year.

While living in Los Angeles, in rather a romantic and providential manner, he made the acquaintance of Lavon Chipman, daughter of John W. Chipman, formerly of American Fork—old settlers and pioneers in that town. The love between Samuel and Lavon was perfectly mutual and in three months from their first acquaintance they were married in the St. George Temple. It was a happy union. They were full of love and congeniality and union with each other. This love and congenial spirit between them never wavered.

Samuel left two sons to perpetuate his name; John Foss and Samuel Parkinson Cowley, (Jr.) with a good mother to train them to walk in the footsteps of their parents, and to bring them up in the fear and admonition of the Lord.

During his service for the Department of Justice he was stationed in several different cities, being moved from one place to another by Mr. J. Edgar Hoover, the head of the department, in accord with the needs of the occasion. He spent several months in each of the following places: Los Angeles; Salt Lake City; Detroit; Chicago; Butte, Montana; and Washington, DC, and latterly again in Chicago. He was constantly improving in ability to perform the functions of his office and calling. He rose from the position of an agent to that of inspector, and ranked third in line of promotion, having only Agent Harold Nathan, standing between him and Mr. Hoover, chief of the FBI. Had he lived to a later date another promotion awaited him in Washington, DC. A special office had been prepared for him with his name upon the door (Marriott letter).

He was the sixth in a group of government men working in the Department of Justice to lay down his life as a martyr to law and justice. He, with his valiant companion, Herman E. Hollis, was slain by vicious assassins on the 27th of November, 1934, at Barrington, Illinois. Hollis died at the place of combat, while Samuel was taken to the Sherman Hospital in Elgin, Illinois, where he passed away at 2:20 am November 28, 1934.

Samuel P. Cowley was honest in every sense of the word. He was courageous and knew no fear. He was moral, temperate, and industrious; possessing a character without a blemish. He was indeed one of God's noblemen.

A few weeks before Samuel's decease he made a hurried trip from Chicago to Los Angeles and return by airplane. He stopped off in Salt Lake City to see his parents and brothers and sisters both going and coming. On his way out he had only two or three hours in the city. He had notified his parents of his coming so that they and Hyde and Matthew met him at the airport. They hurried him to the home of his brother, William Hyde Cowley, where Hyde and his family entertained him. Some of his old time Washington friends were also present; Melrose, Miller, Scott Dahlquist, Llewellen Thomas, and others, besides the members of the family and after a very pleasant visit with Samuel we hurried with him to the airport and off he flew on his last visit to the Pacific Coast.

His mother was then in Los Angeles visiting with our daughter Elna, but she came home before Samuel returned here en route to Chicago. So she saw him in Los Angeles for a very short time. On his return to Salt Lake, his brother Matthew took him to his home, entertained him and his friends and Samuel came here and spent the night at home with us.

He was more than usually appreciative of his parents, very affectionate to his mother, and told how wonderfully he had been treated by his brothers William Hyde Cowley and Matthew Cowley and how he appreciated the same. Had we known and had Samuel known that this was his last earthly visit to us, it could scarcely have been more impressive than it was. And although neither he nor we knew the real import of this visit, we could, when the change came, realize the full meaning of the heavenly spirit that attended Samuel's last visit with us. It was surely a forecast of what was to come in the near future.

A tribute from J. Edgar Hoover, Director, Federal Bureau of Investigation
(SPC, 44)

Samuel P. Cowley entered the service of this division on March 11, 1929. His training prior to his entry into the Division service had been such as to warrant the belief at that time that his rise would be extremely rapid. This belief was found to be amply justified. After serving an investigative apprenticeship in various division offices throughout the country, his talent became so manifest that he was given an executive position. He rose through various executive offices until at the time of his untimely death he held the position of Inspector in the Division of Investigation. And had to his credit the solution of the most important cases handled by the division during the past two years, including those involving John Herbert Dillinger, Charles Arthur 'Pretty Boy' Floyd, and Lester Joseph Gillis, alias 'Baby Face' Nelson.

The loss to the division of the services of so capable an executive official is irreparable. There was further promotion in store for him and I had intended to rely more and more upon his proven ability as time ensued. Not only were his mental attainments superior in almost every line of endeavor, but his personal moral character was above reproach. He possessed an extremely pleasing personality, was modest to an unusual degree, frank, unassuming, simple, earnest and sincere.

As time passes I realize, even more fully that I did at the time of the tragic occurrence in the vicinity of Chicago on November 28, how much both the division and I have lost, not only in the services of a superior executive official, but a friend whose loyalty and friendship possessed a value far beyond material estimate. The heroism reflected in his final battle against murderous gangsters had been referred to so often as to require no comment on my part. It is a tribute not only to Samuel, but to his training, to his faith, and to his associates, who contributed to a greater or lesser extent in the development of his splendid character and personality. I shall always remember him with affection and shall always grieve for his untimely passing.

BIBLIOGRAPHY

Cowley, Lavon. Statement. May, 1987.

Deseret News Magazine, 24 March 1985

"Dillinger Inquest." Associated Press, 23 Jul 1934.

fbi.gov (www)
    A. The Lawless Years
    B. John Paul Chase and Lester M. Gillis
    C. Hall of Honor
    D. The Kansas City Massacre
    E. The New Deal
    F. John Dillinger
    G. The Early Days

geocities.com (www)
    A. John Paul Chase
    B. Final Fight
    C. Deadfall

History of The Church of Jesus Christ of Latter-day Saints. Deseret News Press.

Hoover, J. Edgar. Letter from J. Edgar Hoover to Sam Cowley, July 23, 1934.

Hoover, J. Edgar. *Persons in Hiding.*. Little, Brown and Co., 1938.

Hoover, J. Edgar. *Saga Magazine.* June, 1952.

Hoover, J. Edgar. Statement from J. Edgar Hoover to J. Willard Marriott, head of the Marriott Corporation, May 7, 1958.

nlcomf.com (www). Fallen agents of the FBI.

Herman E. Hollis Memo, 1930.

Nash, Jay Robert. *Dillinger, Dead or Alive.* H. Regnery Co., 1970.

politicalgraveyard.com (www).

Quimby, Myron J. *The Devil's Emissaries.* A. S. Barnes and Co., 1969.

Rossman, W.G. Letter from W. G. Rossman to Lavon Cowley, January 8, 1935.

SPC (Samuel P. Cowley Manuscript Collection). Funeral Tributes. Merrill Library, Utah State University, Logan, Utah.

Toland, John. *The Dillinger Days.* Random House, 1963.

Wisconsin State Journal. Madison, Wisconsin, 19-26 March 1935.

The Magazine of Sigma Chi, Jun. 1935; Oct. 1935; Nov/Dec. 1949; Dec. 1952

ADDITIONAL RESOURCES

American Detective. Oct. 1934; Feb, 1935.

The American Magazine. May, 1936.

The Children's Friend. Mar, 1946.

FBI Investigator. Apr, 1944.

Guideposts. Oct, 1961.

The Improvement Era. Aug, 1935.

The Improvement Era. Oct, 1952.

The Instructor. Aug, 1962.

The Investigator. Apr, 1935.

The Investigator. Apr, 1945.

The Investigator. Jul, 1952.

Millennial Star. Sep, 1959.

Saga. Jun, 1952.

Stag. Jan, 1954.

Startling Detective. Aug, 1935.

The New Era. Feb, 1974.

ACKNOWLEDGMENTS

I am grateful to the following persons and organizations for their contribution to this book:

Betty Barr, River Heights, Utah, who obtained the Samuel P. Cowley manuscript copies from Utah State University.

Dr. Stephen C. Sturgeon, Manuscript Curator, Merrill Library, Utah State University, Logan, Utah, who arranged for the copying of the Cowley manuscript.

Samuel P. Cowley, Jr., Salt Lake City, Utah, younger son of Inspector Cowley, for his generous help in compiling reams of information, for his encouragement in writing this book, and for penning the Forward.

My wife, Helen, for painstakingly examining the manuscript and reviewing content for its improvement.

Sister-in-Law Darlene Cornell, for her diligent efforts in helping with the many revisions of the manuscript.

Todd Kienitz for his invaluable counsel in helping to make me a little more computer literate.

THE AUTHOR

Richard L. Emery wrote for several Midwestern newspapers and radio stations. He graduated from the University of Illinois with a master's degree in political science and is a certified public accountant. He has written several articles for *The Ensign*, and the *Church News*. He lives in Madison, Wisconsin. He is a high priest in The Church of Jesus Christ of Latter-day Saints. He is the father of five children, has 26 grandchildren and eight great-grandchildren. He has served in many callings in the Church, including ward clerk, bishop's counselor, high priests' group leader, stake director of public affairs, and stake executive secretary He with his wife Helen recently served as a senior couple in the California Los Angeles Mission.

Richard has held various positions in state and federal government, including auditor with the Internal Revenue Service and investigator with the Federal Energy Department in the 1970s.